"The magnificence of John [ ] what he gathers up from a range of voices has become in his hand a virtual manifesto. With depth and breadth, he develops what a missional approach to theology looks like. His own constructive work provides a clear and compelling agenda for all to follow. This book is of major importance for both church and academy."

—**George R. Hunsberger**, Western Theological Seminary, Holland, Michigan (emeritus)

"For anyone who wants an excellent introduction to missional theology, its beginnings, its theological and biblical underpinnings, as well as insights regarding its future relevance for the church and the world, this volume is a must-read. Franke offers those new to the missional conversation and those well acquainted with it opportunities to deeply reflect upon and engage (again) the *missio Dei*—what it has meant for missional theology in the past, including its disastrous interpretations due to whiteness and white supremacy, what it means in the present, and its possibilities for the future as the missional theology movement decenters 'those with power,' widens the circle of voices in the conversation, and comes 'prepared to listen rather than to speak.'"

—**Lisa Bowens**, Princeton Theological Seminary

"Just as missional theology is getting hijacked to further pragmatic church growth efforts, Franke provides this outstanding text that encapsulates his previous work while pressing this theological conversation forward. *Missional Theology* is accessible, scholarly, and well-balanced in focus. It should be required reading for anyone invested in God's kingdom, where everyone has enough and no one is afraid."

—**Drew G. I. Hart**, Messiah University; author of *Who Will Be a Witness? Igniting Activism for God's Justice, Love, and Deliverance*

"Franke's *Missional Theology*—equal parts invitation and manifesto—articulates a revolutionary and profoundly life-giving vision of the nature and task of Christian theology. Building on critical areas of theological and missiological consensus, Franke offers a well-reasoned, accessible, and potentially paradigm-shifting argument for a postmodern and postcolonial understanding of mission—rooted in the very nature of God—as the sine qua non for theological reflection. This thoroughgoing revisioning of mission will challenge those who understand mission primarily in terms of evangelism and global outreach as well as those who find missional language to be hopelessly contaminated by Western imperialism and notions of cultural and religious supremacy. Faithfully biblical, inherently ecumenical, and deeply attuned to what the God of all diversity is doing in the world, *Missional Theology* merits a wide readership in churches and theological classrooms."

—**Michael Barram**, Saint Mary's College of California;
author of *Missional Economics: Biblical Justice
and Christian Formation*

"Franke has emerged as one of the second-generation leaders of missional theology. He builds on his teachers' core commitment that the discipline flows out of systematic theology as well as historical and biblical studies. But as this book demonstrates, he is now bringing missional theology more deeply into congregational life and ministry. This is a much-needed next step for the discipline that could have been provided only by a scholar with the heart of a pastor."

—**M. Craig Barnes**, Princeton Theological Seminary

Missional Theology

AN INTRODUCTION

John R. Franke

B
Baker Academic
a division of Baker Publishing Group
Grand Rapids, Michigan

Published by Baker Academic
a division of Baker Publishing Group
PO Box 6287, Grand Rapids, MI 49516-6287
www.bakeracademic.com

Printed in the United States of America

Library of Congress Cataloging-in-Publication Control Number: 2020012718

ISBN 978-0-8010-3635-4 (paperback)
ISBN 978-1-5409-6350-5 (casebound)

20   21   22   23   24   25   26   7   6   5   4   3   2

To Darrell Guder and George Hunsberger,
friends and mentors in missional theology

Contents

Preface

This volume marks both a conclusion and a beginning. As a conclusion, it is the culmination of over a decade of thinking, speaking, and writing on the idea of missional theology. In that time, I have had the opportunity to teach and lecture on the topic at seminaries, colleges, and churches throughout North America as well as other parts of the world. I have experienced firsthand the confusion and misunderstanding that exists among students, church leaders, and the congregations they serve about the term *missional* and its relationship to the church and theology. I have also seen the interest and enthusiasm that emerges when the ideas of missional theology are more clearly grasped and applied to the understanding and practice of Christian witness.

In addition to teaching, I have written on various aspects of missional theology in several books and articles over the years. These include (in chronological order):

"Christian Faith and Postmodern Theory: Theology and the Nonfoundationalist Turn." In *Christianity and the Postmodern Turn*, edited by Myron B. Penner, 105–21. Grand Rapids: Brazos, 2005.

*The Character of Theology: An Introduction to Its Nature,
Task, and Purpose.* Grand Rapids: Baker Academic, 2005.

"God Is Love: The Social Trinity and the Mission of God." In
*Trinitarian Theology for the Church: Scripture, Community,
Worship*, edited by Daniel J. Treier and David E. Lauber,
105–19. Downers Grove, IL: InterVarsity, 2009.

Manifold Witness: The Plurality of Truth. Nashville: Abingdon, 2009.

"Intercultural Hermeneutics and the Shape of Missional
Theology." In *Reading the Bible Missionally*, edited by Michael W. Goheen, 86–103. The Gospel and Our Culture Series. Grand Rapids: Eerdmans, 2016.

"Contextual Mission: Bearing Witness to the Ends of the
Earth." In *Four Views on the Mission of the Church*, edited by Jason Sexton, 107–33. Grand Rapids: Zondervan,
2017.

"Missional Theology: Living God's Love." In *Evangelical Theological Method: Five Views*, edited by Stanley E. Porter and
Steven M. Studebaker, 52–72. Downers Grove, IL: IVP Academic, 2018.

This volume brings together material from all these books and
essays and expands on them to provide (I hope) a clear introduction to missional theology and its basic themes. Thanks to the
publishers of these pieces for granting permission to reproduce
parts of them in this volume.

I intend for this volume to serve as a launching point for further explorations in missional theology, an emerging discipline
that works at the intersections of practical theology, missiology,
and systematic theology in the service of congregational formation for witness. In contrast to those who believe the missional
turn was merely a passing fad, I believe the serious theological,
hermeneutical, spiritual, and ecclesial revolutions spawned by this

conversation have just scratched the surface of their potential. Much more work needs to be done.

For this work to bear the fruit of more informed and faithful witness to the purposes of God in the world, it needs to take root in the life and ministry of local congregations. To that end, I have worked to make this volume as accessible as possible to those who are joining this conversation for the first time, particularly those engaged in, or preparing for, congregational leadership and ministry. Much more can be said on every topic discussed in the book, but in the interest of brevity I resisted the impulse to do so.

When I think of the challenges posed by missional theology, I am reminded of a particular speaking engagement at an evangelical seminary known for its commitment to cross-cultural mission training. Over three days, I gave five lectures on the topics included in this volume. At the end of the series, two members of the faculty responded, a missiologist and a systematic theologian. The missiologist expressed general agreement with my presentation, but the systematic theologian, with grave displeasure, said the lectures contained some of the most dangerous conclusions he had heard in over twenty years of teaching. Afterward, one of the mission students thanked me for lecturing and commented that I sounded more like a missiologist than any theologian he had ever heard. Thinking of the stir I had just created, I replied it was too bad I had not been presented as a missiologist because then nothing I had said would have been deemed controversial. "Yes," the student said, "but then you'd be sitting over in the corner with the rest of us missiologists, who no one really cares about as long as we stay in our lane. But what you're doing is driving the principles of missiology into the disciplines of biblical studies and systematic theology, and that makes people nervous."

Missional theology explores how things might look if mission were moved from the periphery to the center of biblical interpretation, theological construction, congregational life, spiritual formation, and ministerial praxis. This volume is intended to provide a starting place for individuals and communities interested in exploring the possibilities and challenges raised by this missional shift.

Many friends, colleagues, and communities have supported me personally and professionally over the years and directly or indirectly participated in the development of this work. Space and memory do not permit a full recounting here, but I am particularly grateful for two groups of people: the students who have taken my classes in missional theology at six institutions (Biblical Theological Seminary, Evangelische Theologische Faculteit of Leuven, Fuller Theological Seminary, Houston Graduate School of Theology, Princeton Theological Seminary, and Christian Theological Seminary) and the members of two congregations I have served as theologian in residence (First Presbyterian Church of Allentown, Pennsylvania, and Second Presbyterian Church of Indianapolis). I would especially like to mention the members of the Theology, Thoughts, and Coffee class at Second Presbyterian Church who faithfully gather at 8 a.m. on Sundays to discuss these and other matters. My thanks to all the above for their questions, curiosity, and goodwill. This work exists because of them.

Among the many individuals who have encouraged and supported me, I would particularly like to thank Tony Sundermeier, who first encouraged and recruited me to work full time in the church; James Furr, who shares a common vision for missional theology; Michael Barram, my co-conspirator in launching a missional revolution; and the staff at Second Presbyterian Church of Indianapolis, who make it such a wonderful place to work.

Finally, I have had the privilege of working closely with two of the most important leaders in the missional movement of the last twenty years, Darrell Guder and George Hunsberger. With gratitude for their contributions to missional theology and for their mentorship and friendship, I dedicate this volume to them.

1

Missional God

The starting point for missional theology is the notion of a missional God. This means simply that God is, by God's very nature, a missionary God. In a more classical theological rendering, it means mission is an attribute of God. From this perspective, according to South African missiologist David Bosch, "mission is not primarily an activity of the church, but an attribute of God. God is a missionary God."[1] Put another way, in the oft repeated words of renowned German theologian Jürgen Moltmann, "It is not the church that has a mission of salvation to fulfill to the world; it is the mission of the Son and the Spirit through the Father that includes the church, creating a church as it goes on its way."[2]

Affirmations such as these represent one of the most significant developments in the ecumenical movement in the twentieth century. They are shaped by a broad consensus among virtually all

1. David J. Bosch, *Transforming Mission: Paradigm Shifts in Theology of Mission* (Maryknoll, NY: Orbis, 1991), 390.
2. Jürgen Moltmann, *The Church in the Power of the Spirit* (Minneapolis: Fortress, 1993), 64.

theological and ecclesial traditions that participate in ecumenical discourse: that the mission of the church finds its rationale in the *missio Dei*, the mission of God.

Missio Dei

The emergence of *missio Dei* theology is rooted in the history of reflection on the relationship between mission and the church. This reflection was fostered by the International Missionary Council (IMC), which came into being in the aftermath of the 1910 world missionary conference held in Edinburgh and was formally established in 1921. The Edinburgh conference brought together various mission organizations in hopes of fostering better cooperation among them in the task of evangelism, which was generally taken to be synonymous with mission.[3] Mission was assumed to be evangelism, and its practitioners were predominantly Western missionaries connected to Western missionary societies. In that era the tendency was to associate Christianity with the West, distinguishing Christianity from the rest of the non-Christian world. Mission work was understood to be the work of evangelizing the non-Western, non-Christian world. In that context the conference's focus was largely pragmatic, with little reflection on the theological framings of mission.[4]

With the formation of the IMC, theological questions began to emerge, and more forcefully in the aftermath of World War I in which the reputedly Christian nations of the West had attempted to destroy each other. This, coupled with the increasing recession of Christian commitment and the rapid growth of secularism, no doubt hastened by the war, considerably undermined the notion of the "Christian" West. In the midst of these circumstances, a

3. In 1961 the IMC became part of the World Council of Churches as the Commission on World Mission and Evangelism.

4. For a detailed discussion of the Edinburgh conference, see Brian Stanley, *The World Missionary Conference, Edinburgh 1910* (Grand Rapids: Eerdmans, 2009).

new mood prevailed at the IMC conference in Jerusalem in 1928. Debate arose about the traditional notion of mission as little more than the evangelization of non-Christian nations. Questions were raised concerning the significance of social and political action with respect to Christian mission, and about the relationship between the Christian gospel and other religions. While no consensus was reached, the conference significantly altered the shape of the conversation.

As the church and the world faced the challenges of fascism, communism, and a second world war, these questions intensified at subsequent IMC conferences in Tambaram, India (1938), and Whitby, Canada (1947). The language of Christian and non-Christian countries was abandoned, opening the way to new possibilities with respect to the understanding and practice of Christian mission. In the midst of wrestling with these pressing questions, a new imagination concerning the basis for mission slowly began to take shape. The IMC moved from focusing on pragmatic questions concerning the practice of mission to a more basic one: Why mission?

At the 1952 IMC conference in Willingen, Germany, the answer to this question began to take shape with the clear emergence of *missio Dei* theology. While that exact term would not come into vogue until after the conference, the theological assertion was unmistakably indicated. The rationale for mission found its basis in the very nature of God.

The historical impulse for this theological and missiological revolution can be traced to the work of Karl Barth. In a paper presented at the Brandenburg missionary conference in 1932, he articulated an understanding of mission as an activity that finds its first expression in the life of God. Barth and Karl Hartenstein, a contemporary who shared this conviction, began to shape German missiological thinking in the decades that followed the Brandenburg conference, and Hartenstein is credited with coining the term *missio Dei* after the 1952 Willingen conference.

During the centuries preceding the development of *missio Dei* theology, mission had been understood in a variety of ways: in terms of salvation, in which individuals are rescued from eternal condemnation; in terms of culture, in which people from the majority world are introduced to the blessing and privileges of the Christian West; in ecclesial terms, in which the church expands and survives; and in social terms, in which the world is transformed into the kingdom of God by evolutionary or cataclysmic means. "In all of these instances, and in various, frequently conflicting ways, the intrinsic relationship between Christology, soteriology, and the doctrine of the Trinity, so important in the early church, was gradually displaced by one of several versions of the doctrine of grace."[5] From the perspective of the *missio Dei* theology that emerged from Willingen, mission is understood as being derived from the very nature of God. "Willingen's image of mission was mission as participating in the sending of God. Our mission has no life of its own; only in the hands of the sending God can it truly be called mission, not least since the missionary initiative comes from God alone."[6]

From this perspective, mission no longer finds its basis in the church. Instead it is understood as a movement from God to the world, with the church functioning as a participant in that mission. Such participation invests the church in the movement of God's love for the world and calls forth a response of witness and action consistent with that movement. *Missio Dei* theology asserts that God has a particular desire, arising from God's eternal character, to engage with the world. For this reason, the idea of mission is at the heart of the biblical narratives concerning the work of God in human history. It begins with the call to Israel through Abraham to be God's covenant people and the recipients of God's covenant blessings for the purpose of blessing the world:

5. Bosch, *Transforming Mission*, 389.
6. Bosch, *Transforming Mission*, 390.

"Now the LORD said to Abram, 'Go from your country and your kindred and your father's house to the land that I will show you. I will make of you a great nation, and I will bless you, and make your name great, so that you will be a blessing. I will bless those who bless you, and the one who curses you I will curse; and in you all the families of the earth shall be blessed'" (Gen. 12:1–3).

The mission of God is at the heart of the covenant with Israel; it unfolded continuously over the course of the centuries in the life of God's people, as recorded in the narratives of canonical Scripture. This missional covenant reached its revelatory climax in the life, death, and resurrection of Jesus Christ and continues through the sending of the Spirit as the One who calls, guides, and empowers the community of Christ's followers, the church, as the socially, historically, and culturally embodied witness to the gospel of Jesus Christ and the tangible expression of the mission of God. This mission continues today in the global ministry and witness to the gospel of churches in every culture around the world and, guided by the Spirit, moves toward the promised consummation of reconciliation and redemption in the eschaton.

Since Willingen, "the understanding of mission as *missio Dei* has been embraced by virtually all Christian persuasions" starting with Protestants and then by other ecclesial traditions including Eastern Orthodox and Roman Catholic.[7] One of the challenges of this consensus is that, while it inseparably links the mission of the church with participation in the mission of God, there is no specific shared understanding of the precise nature of the church's participation. Attempts to provide such specification have been contested and controversial. However, despite the lack of full conceptual clarity and continued discussion of its theological nuances, "*missio Dei* has become the defining paradigm of mission, being accepted by conciliar and evangelical Protestants, Pentecostals, and both Orthodox and Roman Catholic churches. For almost

7. Bosch, *Transforming Mission*, 390–91.

50 years, the concept has been often reaffirmed, for example by
the World Council of Churches' Commission on World Mission
and Evangelism."[8]

While the connection between the mission of God and the mission of the church remains murky, ecumenical consensus has been
secured on two important points. First, God, by God's very nature,
is a missionary God. Second, the church of this missionary God
must therefore be a missionary church. To elaborate on the first
point, mission is a part of God's very nature and is expressed in
the being and actions of God throughout eternity. This is made
known by the sending of the Son into the world. In the Gospel
of John, Jesus says to his disciples: "Peace be with you. As the
Father has sent me, so I send you" (John 20:21). The term *mission*
is derived from the Latin words "to send" (*mitto*) and "sending"
(*missio*). Mission means to send and be sent. The sending of the
Father and the sentness of the Son and the Spirit point to the being
and action of the triune God as both sender and sent. Mission is
an attribute of God and part of God's very nature.

The second point is connected to the first. There is a distinction between asserting that God has a mission and asserting that
God is, by God's very nature, a missionary. In the first instance,
the action of mission may be incidental to and disconnected from
the being of God; in the second instance, however, the action of
mission is consistent with the very being of God because mission
is one of the divine attributes. A missional church might worship
a God who simply *has* a mission, but it is also possible that such a
God could be worshiped by a church that lacks a missional focus.
On the other hand, if mission is part of God's very nature, then
only a missional church can fully, truly worship such a God. As
Stephen Holmes asserts, a church that refuses the call to mission
is failing to be faithful to the God it worships, in the same way as

8. Mark Laing, "*Missio Dei*: Some Implications for the Church," *Missiology: An
International Review* 37, no. 1 (January 2009): 91.

a church that refuses the command to love. "Just as purposeful, cruciform, self-sacrificial sending is intrinsic to God's own life, being sent in a cruciform, purposeful and self-sacrificial way must be intrinsic to the church being the church."[9]

When viewed from the perspective of *missio Dei* theology, the church's missionary activities can be understood in a new way. Mission in the singular, the mission of God, becomes primary, while the particular mission activities of the church, in the plural, are understood as derivative. In the post-Willingen context, the age of "missions" comes to a conclusion and the age of mission commences. Hence, we distinguish between the mission of God and the mission activities of the church and confess that the latter are authentic only when they faithfully participate in the *missio Dei*. The primary purpose of the mission activity of the church cannot simply be to save souls, or extend the influence of the temporal church, or plant new Christian communities. Instead it must be in continual service to the mission of God in and for the world, as well as against it. "In its mission, the church witnesses to the fullness of the promise of God's reign and participates in the ongoing struggle between that reign and the powers of darkness and evil."[10]

Some have challenged the usefulness of *missio Dei* theology, claiming that it lacks conceptual clarity and noting that some have used it to promote mutually exclusive theological positions. Nevertheless, it has served to articulate the vital point that the basis of mission is neither the church nor any human agent, but the triune God. The church is privileged to participate in this mission, but its basis is found in God.

One of the consequences of affirming that mission is an attribute of God and part of the divine nature is that we also must affirm that the mission of God does not have an end point. It

9. Stephen R. Holmes, "Trinitarian Missiology: Towards a Theology of God as Missionary," *International Journal of Systematic Theology* 8, no. 1 (January 2006): 89.

10. Bosch, *Transforming Mission*, 391.

will not cease at the consummation of the age; it will continue into eternity as an essential aspect of the divine nature. When we conceive of mission in terms of salvation, the church, culture, or social concern, it naturally seems it will have an end when God's creative purposes are fully realized in the eschatological future. However, if mission is an attribute of God, an essential element of the divine character, then it will never come to a conclusion and must continue throughout eternity. This eternal mission has its origin in the life of God who from all eternity has been in an active relationship involving the giving, receiving, and sharing of love between Father, Son, and Holy Spirit. In the words of David Bosch, "God is the fountain of sending love. This is the deepest source of mission. It is impossible to penetrate deeper still."[11] There is mission because God loves.

The Trinity, Love, and the Eternal Mission of God

While the mission of God is complex and multifaceted, its central character, from which all other aspects flow, is love. The idea that God is love is surely one of the most common assumptions of Christians concerning the character of God. This assertion is found repeatedly in the pages of the Bible and has been affirmed regularly throughout the history of the church. But what does it really mean to say that God is love?

When we affirm with Scripture and the Christian tradition that God is love, we are not simply making a statement about the feelings of God toward creation and human beings who are made in God's image. Instead, we are affirming something about the very nature of God's being and actions. God is love for all time—past, present, and future—because God lives eternally in the communal fellowship between Father, Son, and Holy Spirit as they participate in giving, receiving, and sharing love.

11. Bosch, *Transforming Mission*, 392.

Christian theological thinking on the Trinity provides additional support for the assertion that God is love. While the idea of God as Trinity is often viewed as a doctrinal abstraction, closer inspection reveals that it is in fact central to the notion that God is love. In order to understand this, it will be helpful to consider the formation of this basic Christian teaching.

The Bible does not contain an explicit confession of God as triune. Indeed, the term *Trinity* is not part of the scriptural vocabulary, nor is the theological concept developed or fully delineated in the biblical texts. This has caused some to wonder about this teaching and its primacy for Christian faith. It may be helpful, therefore, to think of the doctrine of the Trinity not as an explicit biblical teaching but rather as a theological teaching the early Christians understood as defending central faith convictions they found in the Bible.

By the fourth century the church had come to the conclusion that understanding God as triune was nonnegotiable because it encapsulated the Christian conception of God made known through the life and ministry of Jesus. The early Christian community came to regard confession of the Trinity as necessary on several levels: as an important theological conclusion, as a central component of the faith of the community, and as the definitive Christian affirmation concerning the identity of God. The doctrine was understood as a natural outworking of the faith of the New Testament community.

While the doctrine of the Trinity has often been viewed as a highly abstract and speculative teaching that emerged from the philosophical concerns of third- and fourth-century thinkers, it is more accurate to understand the doctrine as a response to the early Christian community's historical situation. The understanding of God as Trinity emerged and took shape as the followers of Jesus sought to make sense of their beliefs about him and their convictions about God.

It was a response to the challenge of reconciling the inherited commitment to the confession of the one God with the lordship of Jesus Christ and the experience of the Spirit. Far from a philosophical abstraction, the confession of God as triune constitutes the culmination of an attempt on the part of the church to address the central theological question regarding the content of the Christian faith, a question that arose out of the experience of the earliest followers of Jesus. In keeping with their Jewish heritage, the early Christians continued to maintain a core belief in one God. This commitment led them to reject the practices of the surrounding culture of the Roman Empire, which were characterized by belief in many gods. By continuing to declare their commitment to one God, the early Christian community asserted their continuing participation in the covenant that God had initiated with Abraham, who early Christians continued to regard as one of the most important figures in the early history and development of the community.

In this context, the early Christians continued to maintain that there is only one true God, the God of Abraham, Isaac, and Jacob. And this God, they asserted, is the same God as the one revealed in the life and witness of Jesus of Nazareth. This God and only this God is entitled to the worship of the Christian community. The early Christians understood themselves to be the ongoing manifestation of the one people of God, the continuation of the community initiated in the covenant God made with Abraham. Therefore they remained vigorously committed to the monotheistic tradition and practices they saw articulated in the Hebrew Scriptures.

This commitment to monotheism formed a basic assumption around which the early Christians reflected on the events that took place in the life of Jesus of Nazareth. In the midst of their continuation of the Jewish practice of worshiping only one God, the early Christians also came to believe that the one God had come to dwell among them in the person of Jesus of Nazareth. Because of this belief, they ascribed deity to Jesus and worshiped him as the Lord of the universe and the head of their community.

Yet in spite of their commitment to monotheism and the worship of only one God, they also made a clear distinction, following the practice of Jesus himself, between the Son of God and the One whom Jesus addresses as the Father in the Gospel accounts of the Christian canon. While they maintained the divinity of Jesus, they also believed that he is not the same as the Father.

Early Christians also believed that the Holy Spirit is divine. Through the ministry of the Spirit, the followers of Jesus enjoyed an intimate relationship with God and the presence of God in their fellowship and in their own lives. The community believed that through the presence of the Spirit, Christians individually and corporately comprise the temple of God. The affirmation that the work of the Spirit constitutes the Christian community as the temple of God intimately linked the Spirit with God.

The close relationship between the three as God, and the distinctions among them, are evident in the summary formulations found in the New Testament such as Matthew 28:19: "Therefore go and make disciples of all the nations, baptizing them in the name of the Father and of the Son and of the Holy Spirit," and 2 Corinthians 13:14: "May the grace of the Lord Jesus Christ, and the love of God, and the fellowship of the Holy Spirit be with you all."

The challenge of integrating these commitments into a coherent, composite understanding born out of their experience of God led to an emphasis on both the unity and the differentiated plurality of God. The church did not confess three Gods. Yet at the same time, encounters with and experiences of God in the Father, the Son, and the Holy Spirit were far too distinctive to be seen as simply different "modes" of the one God. As a result, the Christian confession of God as triune finds its basis in the practical concern of offering an account of God that reflects the experience of the community and witness of the early believers.

Throughout history the affirmation of the triune character of the divine has provided a framework for Christian thinking about

God and the ongoing development of trinitarian theology. The biblical witness to the early Christian community's experience with God points beyond this temporal encounter to the eternal life of God. The Bible pictures God as acting in the history of the world and also as having a history in which creation is not the beginning point but rather a particular event in the continuing story of the divine life that stretches from the eternal past into the eternal future.

While the acts of God in history are the basis of the doctrine of the Trinity, they are also indicative of God's ongoing internal life. Scripture invites us to think through the implications of this history with respect to the character of God. This suggests a theological principle: God is as God acts. The identity of God is known through the actions of God. The self-revelation of God reflects the character of God. The character and being of God is constituted and made known by God's actions in history.

The revelation of God in Jesus Christ as Father, Son, and Holy Spirit and the actions of Jesus of Nazareth allow us to say that God is as God does, and what God does is love. Through the revelation of God in Jesus Christ we encounter the living embodiment and exposition of God's gracious character, as the One who loves, in relation to humanity. We must set aside all of our assumptions and preconceptions concerning what we already believe to be true of God and instead seek to learn from the God who is, through the actions of God. God is known through what God has done, and what God has done emerges from the person of Jesus Christ and the witness of Scripture. What we see in the life of Jesus and narratives of Scripture is that God is the One who loves. Therefore, as we seek to know the character of God in response to the action of divine self-revelation, we must seek to understand the fundamental biblical assertion that "God is love" (1 John 4:8, 16).

We should not presume that what we already believe about the character of love, based on particular individual or generally accepted cultural assumptions, applies to the love of God. Rather, our knowledge of the love of God should be shaped by the particular way in which God loves through the ongoing establishment of communion between God and God's creatures in and through Jesus.

God's love for the world is not that of an uninvolved, unmoved, passionless Deity. It is the love of one who is actively and passionately involved in the ongoing drama of life in the world, and who lavishly pours out this love in Jesus Christ. This lavish expression of love for humanity and creation, revealed in Jesus Christ, points us to the internal life of God as an eternal trinitarian fellowship of love shared between Father, Son, and Holy Spirit. In other words, explication of the triune God in God's self-disclosure in and to creation is at the same time the explication of the triune God in the divine reality. In summarizing this story, the Christian tradition affirms that from all eternity past and into the eternal future, God has been and will be in an active, loving relationship characterized by the giving, receiving, and sharing of love between Father, Son, and Holy Spirit.

This relationship includes both difference and unity. This eternal fellowship of divine love is characterized by both unity-in-plurality and plurality-in-unity in which we affirm that the one God exists in three distinct persons (to use the classical language)—Father, Son, and Holy Spirit—and that the three together are the one God. Difference and otherness are part of the divine life throughout eternity. While Father, Son, and Holy Spirit together are one God, their unity is not an outgrowth of sameness. Rather, they are one in the very midst of their difference.

Perhaps the single most significant development in twentieth-century trinitarian theology has been the broad consensus that relationality is the most helpful way to understand the Trinity. This so-called relational turn is viewed as an alternative to the ontology of substance that dominated theological reflection on the Trinity throughout much of church history.

14

The traditional understanding of the Trinity placed emphasis on an abstract property of substance or a divine essence. This substantialist conception carried within itself the distinction between absolute essence and relational attributes. According to this understanding, essence is absolute, and therefore it must remain unchanged in order to preserve its identity. If change occurs in the essence of an entity, its identity is lost. Relationality, in turn, was deemed to belong to the dimension of attributes, not substance. Consequently, substantialist theologians suggested that God is absolute and immutable in the essential divine nature, while maintaining relationality to creation through the divine attributes. What could not be allowed in the classical tradition is the notion that the divine essence is somehow contingent on the relational dimensions of its life.

In much of the classical literature on the nature of God, this perspective obscured God's internal relationality and God's loving relationship to creation. Theologians today routinely critique the concept as implying that God is an isolated, solitary individual. At the heart of this critique is the apparent incompatibility of this idea of an eternal, essentially immutable God with the portrait in the biblical narratives of a God who has entered into loving relationship with creation. Although debate continues regarding the degree to which the category of substance ought to be abandoned, theologians voice considerable agreement that the primary accent should be placed on the category of relationality. Catherine LaCugna, to cite one example, asserts that *person* rather than *substance* is the primary ontological category, noting that the ultimate source of reality is not a "by-itself" or an "in-itself" but a person, a "toward-another." She concludes that the triune God is "self-communicating" and exists from all eternity "in relation to another."[12]

12. Catherine Mowry LaCugna, *God for Us: The Trinity and Christian Life* (San Francisco: HarperCollins, 1991), 14–15.

Elizabeth Johnson claims that the priority of relation in the triune God challenges and critiques classical theism's concentration on "singleness" in God; because the persons are "constituted by their relationships to each other, each is unintelligible except as connected with the others." This assertion leads Johnson to the conclusion that the "very principle of their being" is to be found in the category of relation.[13] Similarly, Robert Jenson notes that the original thrust of trinitarian thought was that God's relations to us are internal to the triune life and that it is "in carrying out this insight that the 'relation' concept was introduced to define the distinction of identities."[14] David Cunningham notes that the breadth of the current consensus about the priority of relationality in trinitarian discourse is evidenced by the fact that one can cite both Jenson and Johnson in support of it, even though the two thinkers "are not usually noted for being in close agreement with one another."[15]

This theological consensus encompasses a diverse variety of thinkers including such luminaries as John Zizioulas, Jürgen Moltmann, Wolfhart Pannenberg, Leonardo Boff, Colin Gunton, Alan Torrance, Millard Erickson, and Stanley Grenz. While they may differ from each other on the precise construction of relationality within the life of God, they have all followed the relational turn.

In addition to the consensus among contemporary theologians, Veli-Matti Kärkkäinen states that the "move to relationality is also in keeping with the dynamic understanding of reality and the human being as well as human community in late modernity." He notes that the ideas of isolation, individualism, and

13. Elizabeth A. Johnson, *She Who Is: The Mystery of God in Feminist Theological Discourse* (New York: Crossroad, 1992), 216.
14. Robert W. Jenson, *The Triune Identity: God According to the Gospel* (Philadelphia: Fortress, 1982), 120.
15. David S. Cunningham, *These Three Are One: The Practice of Trinitarian Theology* (Malden, MA: Blackwell, 1998), 26.

independence are products of modernist thought-forms. "Over against the typical modernist bias to classify and categorize everything into distinct units [only think of the methods of the natural sciences], postmodernity speaks of relationality, interdependence, becoming, emerging, and so on. In this changing intellectual atmosphere, the value of communion theology is being appreciated in a new way."[16] Stanley Grenz speaks of this relational turn as envisioning a move "from the one subject to the three persons" with respect to our understanding of God.[17] In other words, God is social, not solitary.

Understanding God as relational plurality rather than a solitary being raises a crucial question: What does it mean to affirm that God is one? In John's Gospel, Jesus says, "I and the Father are one" (10:30) and explains that his works were done so that those who saw them might "know and understand that the Father is in me and I am in the Father" (10:38). In seeking to explain this, thinkers in the early church turned to an idea known as *perichoresis*. This refers to the mutual interdependence of Father, Son, and Holy Spirit in their trinitarian relation with one another. It seeks to explain the nature of the divine life with the assertion that while the three members of the Trinity remain wholly distinct from each other, they are also bound together in such a way that the Father, Son, and Spirit are dependent on each other for their very identities as Father, Son, and Spirit. In other words, the Father, Son, and Spirit would not be who they are—that is, would not be God—apart from the interdependent relationality they share with each other.

This relational interdependence is manifested in the earthly life of Jesus, who did not function as an autonomous, independent individual. Rather, he says that he constantly seeks the will of the

16. Veli-Matti Kärkkäinen, *The Trinity: Global Perspectives* (Louisville: Westminster John Knox, 2007), 387.

17. Stanley J. Grenz, *The Social God and the Relational Self: A Trinitarian Theology of the Imago Dei* (Louisville: Westminster John Knox, 2001), 23–57.

Father and that he can do nothing by himself but only what he sees the Father doing. At the same time, he also says that the Father judges no one but has entrusted all judgment to the Son. Nevertheless, in rendering these judgments he says, "I can do nothing on my own. As I hear, I judge; and my judgment is just, because I seek to do not my own will but the will of him who sent me" (John 5:30).

This understanding of perichoresis leads to the conclusion that the Father, Son, and Holy Spirit are one by virtue of their interdependent relationality. The contemporary consensus concerning the relationality of the life of God brings us back to the affirmation that God is love. Articulating the doctrine of the Trinity in accordance with the category of relationality gives us an indication as to how this biblical and classical assertion is to be comprehended. From the beginning and throughout all of eternity, the life of the triune God has been and continues to be characterized by love. Love is an especially fruitful term for comprehending the life of God since it is an inherently relational concept. It requires both subject and object. Because God is a triune plurality-in-unity and unity-in-plurality, God comprehends both love's subject and love's object. For this reason, when viewed theologically, the statement "God is love" refers primarily to the eternal, relational intratrinitarian fellowship among Father, Son, and Holy Spirit.

The interdependent relationality of the divine life coupled with the presence of difference and otherness leads to the conclusion that the love of God is not an assimilating love. This love does not seek to make that which is different the same. Rather, God lives in harmonious fellowship with the other through the active relations of self-sacrificing, self-giving love.

The love that characterizes the life of God from all eternity is the basis for God's actions in the world; they flow from the fellowship of self-sacrificial love God has enjoyed throughout eternity. As Stephen Holmes puts it, "Purposeful, self-sacrificial acts of loving concern flowing from the Father through the Son and Spirit to the world God has created are fundamental images of who God is, from all eternity."[18] The love that characterizes the mission of God from all eternity is the compelling basis for the extension of the divine mission to the world. It is to the mission of God as it is expressed in the world that we now turn our attention.

The Mission of God in the World

From the perspective of the eternal mission of God, creation can be understood as a reflection of God's expansive love, whereby the triune God brings into being another reality, that which is not God, and establishes a relationship of love, grace, and blessing for the purpose of drawing that reality into participation in the divine fellowship of love. In this way the love of God expands beyond Father, Son, and Holy Spirit to include others.

However, even though human beings are created in the image of God, they rebelled against the love of God and others. Instead of seeking the well-being of their fellow humans, they have sought their own good at the expense of others and established oppressive societies that colonize and marginalize citizens, particularly the powerless and vulnerable. This activity, along with the dispositions of the intellect, the will, and emotions that bring it into fruition, is what Scripture calls sin.

This activity created enmity among the peoples of the earth. From the perspective of the Jewish tradition, a focal point of this enmity is the relationship between Jews and gentiles. In response to this human rebellion and the resulting hostility among the people of the earth, God sends Jesus the Son into the world: "For God so loved the world that he gave his only Son, so that everyone who believes in him may not perish but may have eternal life. Indeed, God did not send the Son into the world to condemn

18. Holmes, "Trinitarian Missiology," 88.

the world, but in order that the world might be saved through him" (John 3:16–17). The Son is sent into the world to redeem it through a cruciform life of humility, service, obedience, and death for the sake of others: "Let the same mind be in you that was in Christ Jesus, who, though he was in the form of God, did not regard equality with God as something to be exploited, but emptied himself, taking the form of a slave, being born in human likeness. And being found in human form, he humbled himself and became obedient to the point of death—even death on a cross" (Phil. 2:5–8).

By his teaching and example, Jesus called the world to follow his way of life and participate in the kingdom of God, a community of love where everyone has enough and no one needs to be afraid. The Spirit is sent into the world to call, guide, and empower the community of Christ's followers in their missional vocation to be the people of God in the particular social, historical, and cultural circumstances in which they are situated. Through the witness of the church to the good news of God's love and mission, the Spirit calls forth a new community from every tribe and nation, centered on Jesus Christ, to be a provisional demonstration of God's will for all creation and empowers it to live God's love for the sake of the world.

This missional pattern, manifested in the world through the sending of the Son and the sending of the Spirit out of love for the world, is lived out and expressed in the context of the eternal community of love; it points to the missional character of God, who seeks to extend the love shared by Father, Son, and Holy Spirit into the created order. Before giving attention to a more detailed summary of the mission of the church, it will be helpful to keep in mind the focal point of the mission of God as it moves from God's life and into the world through Jesus and the Spirit. Flowing out of the divine life in trinity, love is central to the mission of God in the world. When asked which commandment is the greatest, Jesus replies: "You shall love the Lord your God with all your heart, and

with all your soul, and with all your mind. This is the greatest and
first commandment. And a second is like it: 'You shall love your
neighbor as yourself.' On these two commandments hang all the
law and the prophets" (Matt. 22:37–40).

In 1 John 4:7–12, the primacy of love is underscored in the
relationship of God to the church:

> Beloved, let us love one another, because love is from God; everyone
> who loves is born of God and knows God. Whoever does not love
> does not know God, for God is love. God's love was revealed among
> us in this way: God sent his only Son into the world so that we
> might live through him. In this is love, not that we loved God but
> that he loved us and sent his Son to be the atoning sacrifice for our
> sins. Beloved, since God loved us so much, we also ought to love
> one another. No one has ever seen God; if we love one another,
> God lives in us, and his love is perfected in us.

Above all things, the church is called to bear witness to the love
of God for the world by imitating the life of Christ and living
God's love. From this perspective, love is the central expression
of Christian faith and extends even to our enemies. In the words
of Jesus found in Matthew 5:43–45, "You have heard that it was
said, 'You shall love your neighbor and hate your enemy.' But I
say to you, Love your enemies and pray for those who persecute
you, so that you may be children of your Father in heaven; for he
makes his sun rise on the evil and on the good, and sends rain on
the righteous and on the unrighteous."

Because the church worships the missional God who is love,
the church must love all people, including those who are enemies.
Nothing less than its witness to the gospel is at stake. If the church
ignores this most basic calling or fails to live it out in the world, it
is not characterized as a community of faithful disciples of Jesus
Christ and is not practicing Christian faith, no matter what else it
may do. Paul makes this point abundantly clear in 1 Corinthians
13:1–8:

> If I speak in the tongues of mortals and of angels, but do not have love, I am a noisy gong or a clanging cymbal. And if I have prophetic powers, and understand all mysteries and all knowledge, and if I have all faith, so as to remove mountains, but do not have love, I am nothing. If I give away all my possessions, and if I hand over my body so that I may boast, but do not have love, I gain nothing. Love is patient; love is kind; love is not envious or boastful or arrogant or rude. It does not insist on its own way; it is not irritable or resentful; it does not rejoice in wrongdoing, but rejoices in the truth. It bears all things, believes all things, hopes all things, endures all things. Love never ends. But as for prophecies, they will come to an end; as for tongues, they will cease; as for knowledge, it will come to an end.

As an outworking of divine love, the mission of God is expressed in the world through the life of Jesus and the witness of the Spirit as salvation. Paul writes in his letter to the Romans: "For I am not ashamed of the gospel; it is the power of God for salvation to everyone who has faith, to the Jew first and also to the Greek" (1:16). As Paul makes clear in the letter, the means of that salvation is the life, death, and resurrection of Jesus Christ, who is the Son of God and the Lord of the world.

This salvation entails the liberation of the created order—humanity and the entire cosmos—from the powers of sin and death (Rom. 8:2–25). In the same way that the mission of God in Jesus Christ to love the world is passed on to the church, so the mission of salvation and reconciliation is entrusted to the church: "All this is from God, who reconciled us to himself through Christ, and has given us the ministry of reconciliation; that is, in Christ God was reconciling the world to himself, not counting their trespasses against them, and entrusting the message of reconciliation to us. So we are ambassadors for Christ, since God is making his appeal through us; we entreat you on behalf of Christ, be reconciled to God" (2 Cor. 5:18–20). As participants in the mission of God in the world, the church shares not only in the love of God but in the work of salvation as well.

When speaking of salvation, it is important not to approach it from the individualistic perspective of modern Western culture. From this perspective, salvation has often been viewed primarily as the redemption of particular individuals for a heavenly future. To read the biblical witness in this way is to miss the full scope and grandeur of the divine mission. God's actions are on behalf of the whole created order so that it will be set free from its bondage to decay.

The cosmic scope of this mission is captured in the words of Beverly Roberts Gaventa, who writes that, according to Paul in Romans, the mission of God involves the work of rescuing the whole world "from the powers of Sin and Death so that a newly created humanity—Jew and Gentile—is released for the praise of God in community."[19] A focal point of this salvation is the realization of peace on earth. In the New Testament, a significant element of this vision is focused on the inclusion of the gentiles in the family of God. Ephesians asserts that the establishment of this inclusive community is part of the eternal purpose of God to establish peace in the world.[20] According to Ephesians 1:9–10, God "has made known to us the mystery of his will, according to his good pleasure that he set forth in Christ, as a plan for the fullness of time, to gather up all things in him, things in heaven and things on earth." Michael Gorman observes that in Ephesians 2 we see that the mystery referred to here is made known in the gospel and is "best characterized with respect to humanity as a divine peace mission."[21]

19. Beverly Roberts Gaventa, "The Mission of God in Paul's Letter to the Romans," in *Paul as Missionary: Identity, Activity, Theology, and Practice*, ed. Trevor J. Burke and Brian S. Rosner, Library of New Testament Studies 420 (London: T&T Clark, 2011), 65–66.

20. For a detailed interpretation of Ephesians as a call to participate in the peace of God, see Michael J. Gorman, *Becoming the Gospel: Paul, Participation, and Mission*, The Gospel and Our Culture Series (Grand Rapids: Eerdmans, 2015), 181–211.

21. Gorman, *Becoming the Gospel*, 188.

This divine plan is intended to restore harmony to creation by bringing unity to that which is currently scattered and fragmented. This is the power of God working through Christ and the church, which is Christ's body on earth: "God put this power to work in Christ when he raised him from the dead and seated him at his right hand in the heavenly places, far above all rule and authority and power and dominion, and above every name that is named, not only in this age but also in the age to come. And he has put all things under his feet and has made him the head over all things for the church, which is his body, the fullness of him who fills all in all" (Eph. 1:20–23). Commenting on this in the context of a detailed exegesis of Ephesians, Gorman writes: "The church, as described briefly here and in more detail in the rest of the letter, is intended by God to be a foretaste of the future cosmic peace and harmony that has been the eternal divine plan."[22] This is summarized in Ephesians 3:8–11:

> Although I am the very least of all the saints, this grace was given to me to bring to the Gentiles the news of the boundless riches of Christ, and to make everyone see what is the plan of the mystery hidden for ages in God who created all things; so that through the church the wisdom of God in its rich variety might now be made known to the rulers and authorities in the heavenly places. This was in accordance with the eternal purpose that he has carried out in Christ Jesus our Lord.

Ephesians 2 articulates the consequences of the work of God in Christ to bring reconciliation between Jew and gentile, and therefore the world. Through Christ, Jew and gentile have been made one and the dividing wall of hostility has been broken down (v. 14); one new humanity has emerged in place of two, bringing peace to the world (v. 15); both groups have been reconciled, putting hostility to death (v. 16); both groups participate in the Spirit and have

22. Gorman, *Becoming the Gospel*, 189.

access to God (v. 18); Jew and gentile are no longer strangers and aliens to one another (v. 19). Through Christ and the Spirit, Jews and gentiles are members together in the family of God.

Peace and harmony in the world are central to the mission of God. For the church in the context of the ancient world, this meant peace between Jew and gentile. For the church in the context of Christian Europe, it meant peace among competing Christian communities. For the church at the outset of the third millennium, it means peace among the religions of the world. Apart from such religious peace, there is no hope for the peace God intends for the world.

The good news of the gospel is peace in the world and the end of the violence and hostility that leads to death. This is a fundamental part of the message of salvation. Hence, the communities of those who follow Jesus are exhorted in Ephesians 4:1–3 "to lead a life worthy of the calling to which you have been called, with all humility and gentleness, with patience, bearing with one another in love, making every effort to maintain the unity of the Spirit in the bond of peace." Commenting on this broad conception of the divine mission of salvation, Gorman observes: "God is therefore at work creating an international network of multicultural, socio-economically diverse communities ('churches') that participate in this liberating, transformative reality *now*—even if incompletely and imperfectly."[23]

The New Testament uses numerous words, images, and phrases to articulate a comprehensive vision of God's mission of salvation including liberation, transformation, new creation, peace, reconciliation, and justification.[24] This salvific mission is rooted in the self-giving, self-sacrificing love of God expressed in the eternal trinitarian fellowship and made known in the created order through the life, death, and resurrection of Jesus Christ. It is this

23. Gorman, *Becoming the* Gospel, 24–25.
24. Gorman, *Becoming the Gospel*, 25.

divine mission that forms the context for an understanding of the mission of the church.

Before focusing more specifically on the mission of the church, let us look at the conclusion of Matthew's Gospel and consider the means by which God intends to accomplish this mission. These verses of Matthew's Gospel have come to be known as the Great Commission—to make disciples of all the nations: "Now the eleven disciples went to Galilee, to the mountain to which Jesus had directed them. When they saw him, they worshiped him; but some doubted. And Jesus came and said to them, 'All authority in heaven and on earth has been given to me. Go therefore and make disciples of all nations, baptizing them in the name of the Father and of the Son and of the Holy Spirit, and teaching them to obey everything that I have commanded you. And remember, I am with you always, to the end of the age'" (28:16–20). Before turning specifically to the content of this commission, let us note that it is framed within the lordship of Jesus—"all authority in heaven and on earth has been given to me"—and the presence of Jesus—"I am with you always, to the end of the age." This is a crucial reminder that the commission given here proceeds by the power and presence of God. Throughout history, the followers of Jesus who have been baptized into solidarity with him and have therefore inherited this commission have not been left to fulfill it on our own—the Lord is with us in this work, and ultimately it belongs to God, not us.

In order to understand the content of the commission Jesus gives here to his disciples and by extension to the church, it will be helpful to know something about the nature and structure of Matthew's Gospel. It has particularly deep roots in Judaism. While this is true of all the Gospels and the New Testament generally, it is especially true of Matthew. Scholars have long noted that five distinct sections give overall shape to the work. This fivefold structure reflects the Pentateuch, the foundational document of Judaism. At the heart of the Pentateuch are God's covenant with Abraham; the story of Moses and the exodus from Egypt; the creation of a new community under God; and the giving of the laws by which the community was to live. The fivefold structure of Matthew implies that the story of Jesus is analogous to the ancient story of Israel.

These connections show up in many of the details found in Matthew. For instance, the teaching material contained in chapters 5–7 is known as the Sermon on the Mount—yet Matthew is the only Gospel that says Jesus taught this from a mountain. In Matthew's account, Jesus is pictured as a new Moses, revealing God's will from a new Sinai indicative of the Gospel's central theme: Jesus as a new Moses leading a new exodus from a new pharaoh (the Roman emperor) into a new way of life in keeping with the covenant God made with Abraham. This background has led scholars to note the correlation between the Great Commission in Matthew 28 and God's covenant with Abraham in Genesis 12:1–3, "Go . . . I will make of you a great nation . . . so that you will be a blessing. . . . And in you all the families of the earth shall be blessed." The two commissions are indivisibly linked, showing that the Jesus story is intended as a continuation of Israel's story with a common concern: the creation of a new community formed by God's love and committed to the establishment of that love throughout the earth in order to bring about a new world—a world where the will of God is done on earth as in heaven.

In the Hebrew tradition, this vision of a new world is profoundly captured in the words of the prophet Isaiah. It will be a world in which

> No more shall the sound of weeping be heard . . .
>   or the cry of distress.
> No more shall there be in it
>   an infant that lives but a few days,
>   or an old person who does not live out a lifetime. . . .
> They shall not build and another inhabit;
>   they shall not plant and another eat;

> for like the days of a tree shall the days of my people be,
>   and my chosen shall long enjoy the work of their
>   hands.
> They shall not labor in vain,
>   or bear children for calamity. . . .
> The wolf and the lamb shall feed together,
>   the lion shall eat straw like the ox. (65:19–25)

This is a vision of an alternative to the reality we see around us—a vision of a world where everyone has enough and no one needs to be afraid. This is the world God intended from the beginning.

However, as stated previously, human beings have rebelled against God's intentions and sought their own good at the expense of others. In response, God made a covenant with Abraham and called a people to bless the nations of the world. God sent Jesus into the world to bless the nations and bring about salvation through his life, teachings, and death. But the death of Jesus is not the end of the story. Instead, leading New Testament scholar N. T. Wright describes the death of Jesus as "the day the revolution began."[25] Jesus institutes a covenant of vocation whereby he commissions his followers to go to the nations and make disciples who will follow his way of life and create a new world, the realization of Isaiah's vision, the kingdom of God—here and now, on this earth.

This is God's mission, not ours, and we are dependent on the power and presence of God for its fulfillment. That said, it is also important to understand that God has chosen us to share in this work; to be sure, it will not happen without God, but neither will it happen without our faithful participation. We are called not just to believe the gospel, not just to believe in Jesus, but to become the gospel by being disciples of Jesus. We share in God's life by sharing in God's work of bringing about the world God intends.

25. N. T. Wright, *The Day the Revolution Began: Reconsidering the Meaning of Jesus's Crucifixion* (San Francisco: HarperOne, 2016).

Hence, the mission of the church needs to reflect the scope and
size of God's intentions for the world. What might this look like?

The next chapter will offer a fuller delineation, but here it will
help to mention the five marks of mission—a particularly prominent summary of the mission of the church articulated by the
Anglican Communion. While these marks are not a comprehensive
definition of mission, they are rich with significance and point
effectively to the holistic scope of God's work in the world.

> *Evangelism*: to proclaim the good news of God's kingdom
> *Formation*: to teach, baptize, and nurture new believers
> *Compassion*: to respond to human need by loving service
> *Justice*: to seek to transform unjust structures of society
> *Creation care*: to strive to safeguard the integrity of creation
> and sustain and renew the life of the earth.[26]

All of these intrinsically flow from commitment to the lordship
of Jesus and the establishment of the kingdom of God, a new
world where everyone will have enough and no one will need to
be afraid. The realization of this vision accounts for Jesus's commission to his followers at the end of Matthew's Gospel to go and
make disciples of the nations, teaching them to obey everything he
commanded—the ways of the kingdom. The making of disciples
is God's plan for creating a new world and establishing the kingdom of God. In other words, it is an intrinsic part of the mission
of God in the world. Missionary theologian Lesslie Newbigin has
articulated the centrality of Christian congregational formation
for the work of God in the world, suggesting that the church is
the primary reality that needs to be accounted for and developed
if we are to see a demonstrable Christian impact on public life in
an increasingly secular world.

26. Andrew Walls and Cathy Ross, eds., *Mission in the Twenty-First Century:
Exploring the Five Marks of Global Mission* (Maryknoll, NY: Orbis, 2008).

In making this assertion, Newbigin does not discount the importance of the numerous activities—such as conferences, evangelistic work, and the distribution of Bibles and Christian literature—Christians use to engage public life with the claims and implications of the gospel. While these are significant and worthwhile, he maintains they are ultimately of secondary importance and only have power to accomplish the purposes for which they are intended as they arise from, are firmly rooted in, and lead inextricably back to a believing community. He writes, "How is it possible that the gospel should be credible, that people should come to believe that the power which has the last word in human affairs is represented by a man hanging on a cross? I am suggesting that the only answer, the only hermeneutic of the gospel, is a congregation of men and women who believe it and live by it."[27]

This type of all-encompassing, interdependent, individual and communal formation is precisely what is called for in the New Testament as participation in the mission of God. It is discipleship in the way of Jesus that has the capacity to change the world and bring about God's intentions. However, it is a slow process that requires long-standing faithfulness in the face of difficult and seemingly insurmountable circumstances. This is why Jesus compares the kingdom to a mustard seed: "The kingdom of heaven is like a mustard seed that someone took and sowed in his field; it is the smallest of all the seeds, but when it has grown it is the greatest of shrubs and becomes a tree, so that the birds of the air come and make nests in its branches" (Matt. 13:31–32). The growth of the kingdom is slow and sometimes even imperceptible, but in time it produces a harvest of righteousness.

David Bosch concludes that the comprehensive nature of the divine mission demands a more integral and holistic understanding of the character of salvation, and therefore of the mission of the

27. Lesslie Newbigin, *The Gospel in a Pluralist Society* (Grand Rapids: Eerdmans, 1989), 227.

church, than has traditionally been the case: "Salvation is as coherent, broad, and deep as the needs and exigencies of human
existence. Mission therefore means being involved in the ongoing dialogue between God, who offers salvation, and the world,
which—enmeshed in all kinds of evil—craves that salvation."[28] It
is this divine mission that shapes the vocation of the church sent
into the world to continue the work of Jesus. As he was sent, so
he sends the church.

28. Bosch, *Transforming Mission*, 400.

2

Missional Church

The extension of the mission of God into the created order occurs not only through the sending of the Son and the Spirit but also in the sending of the church. As David Bosch observes, this biblical pattern demonstrates that mission is derived from the very nature of God and must be situated in the context of the doctrine of the Trinity rather than ecclesiology or soteriology. From this perspective, the classical doctrine of the *missio Dei* expressed as God the Father sending the Son, and the Father and the Son sending the Spirit, may be expanded "to include yet another 'movement': Father, Son, and Spirit sending the church into the world."[1]

In keeping with the pattern of this sending, the mission of the church is intimately connected with the mission of God in the sending of Jesus and the Spirit. The church is called to be the image of God, the body of Christ, and the dwelling place of the Spirit in the world as it represents and extends the good news of

1. David J. Bosch, *Transforming Mission: Paradigm Shifts in Theology of Mission* (Maryknoll, NY: Orbis, 1991), 390.

God's love for the world as a sign, instrument, and foretaste of the kingdom of God. Before turning our attention to the mission of the church, let us briefly summarize the major points from the previous chapter.

God is love. God lives from all eternity in an interactive relationship characterized by the giving, receiving, and sharing of love between Father, Son, and Holy Spirit. Together these three are one God by virtue of their interdependent relationality.

God is a missionary God. Mission is a part of God's very nature. It is expressed in the being and actions of God throughout eternity and made known by the sending of the Son into the world. The church of this God must be missionary because it worships a missionary God.

Difference and otherness are part of the divine life. While Father, Son, and Holy Spirit together are one God, their unity is not an outgrowth of sameness. Rather, they are one in the very midst of their difference.

The love of God is not an assimilating love. The love of God does not seek to make that which is different the same; rather, God lives in harmonious fellowship with the other through the active relations of self-sacrificing, self-giving love.

Creation is a manifestation of the expansive love of God. God seeks to extend the love shared and expressed in the divine life by bringing into being another reality, that which is not God, with the intention of drawing the created order to participate in the divine fellowship of love.

Human beings, created in the image of God, have rebelled against the love of God. Instead of seeking the well-being of their fellow humans, they have sought their own good at the expense of others and established oppressive societies that colonize and marginalize citizens, particularly the powerless and vulnerable.

Jesus is sent into the world to bring about salvation. Jesus is not sent to condemn the world but to redeem it through a life of humility, service, obedience, death, and resurrection for the sake of others. By his teaching and example, he called the world to follow his way of life and participate in the kingdom of God, a community in which everyone has enough and no one needs to be afraid. By his death and resurrection, he conquered the powers of sin and death, reconciling the world with God.

The Spirit is sent into the world to call, guide, and empower the followers of Jesus to continue his revolutionary mission. The Spirit calls forth a new community from every tribe and nation, centered on Jesus Christ, and empowers it to live God's love for the world and continue his revolutionary mission of proclaiming and establishing the kingdom of God.

These commitments provide the theological background for understanding the mission of the church, which is a community sent into the world as a continuation of the mission of God. As Jesus is sent, so he sends the church as a sign, instrument, and foretaste of the kingdom of God.[2] As such, the historical and contemporary embodiments of the church are local outposts of God's universal mission.

In the previous chapter we looked briefly at Matthew 28 in conjunction with the mission of God. In seeking to understand the mission of the church in relation to the mission of God, we begin our exploration with the words of Jesus in John 20:21–23: "Jesus said to them again, 'Peace be with you. As the Father has sent me, so I send you.' When he had said this, he breathed on them and said to them, 'Receive the Holy Spirit. If you forgive the sins of any, they are forgiven them; if you retain the sins of any, they are retained.'" Here the disciples, representing the church, are sent into the world by Jesus after the pattern by which the Father sent the Son. They are called to continue his work.

---

2. The notion of the church as a sign, instrument, and foretaste of the kingdom of God is drawn from the work of Lesslie Newbigin, *Foolishness to the Greeks: The Gospel and Western Culture* (Grand Rapids: Eerdmans, 1986), 124.

This sending is at the very core of the church's reason and purpose for being and must shape all that the church is and does. Mission must not be viewed as merely one of the many programs of the church or something done by a few specially called people who proclaim the gospel in faraway lands. In the words of the authors of *Missional Church*, mission "defines the church as God's sent people. Either we are defined by mission, or we reduce the scope of the gospel and the mandate of the church. Thus our challenge today is to move from church with mission to missional church."[3] Since the publication of that book in 1998, the term *missional church* has become commonplace in theological and praxis-oriented conversations about the nature of the church in a social climate that is decidedly and increasingly post-Christian. Indeed, the notion of the missional church has become ubiquitous, spawning numerous conversations, networks, programs, and publications seeking to capture the dynamism inherent in the idea.[4]

The close and indissoluble link between the mission of the Son and the mission of the church is established in John 20:21–23 in two ways. The first is by the gift of the promised Spirit who anointed Jesus for his mission at his baptism in the Jordan; now this same Spirit will guide and empower the church as it continues the mission of Jesus. Second, it is established by Jesus entrusting to the church the authority that was central to his mission—the authority to forgive sins.

Lesslie Newbigin points out that this scene communicates more than simply the general idea that God forgives sin. Rather,

3. Darrell L. Guder, ed., *Missional Church: A Theological Vision for the Sending of the Church in North America* (Grand Rapids: Eerdmans, 1998), 6. While Guder served as the project coordinator and editor of the volume, it was cowritten by a team of authors including, in addition to Guder, Lois Barrett, Inagrace T. Dieterrich, George R. Hunsberger, Alan J. Roxburgh, and Craig Van Gelder.

4. The breadth of the missional church conversation has been surveyed and assessed in Craig Van Gelder and Dwight J. Zscheile, *The Missional Church in Perspective: Mapping Trends and Shaping the Conversation* (Grand Rapids: Baker Academic, 2011).

it conveys the specific commission to do something that would otherwise not be done in the world—namely, "to bring the forgiveness of God to actual men and women in their concrete situations in the only way that it can be done so long as we are in the flesh—by the word and act and gesture of another human being."[5] It is the forgiveness of sins that makes possible the gift of God's peace. The restoration of peace or shalom, the all-embracing blessing of the God of Israel and Jesus Christ, may be the simplest, most compelling, and most comprehensive way of articulating the content of the commission given to the church. It is the focus of the initial word of Jesus to his disciples: "Peace be with you" (20:19). This peace that Jesus speaks to his disciples is one of the most central elements of the presence of God's kingdom in the created order, and perhaps its most telling mark. "The church is a movement launched into the life of the world to bear in its own life God's gift of peace for the life of the world. It is sent, therefore, not only to proclaim the kingdom but to bear in its own life the presence of the kingdom."[6]

The mission of the church encompasses both the character of its internal communal life and its external activities in the world. This comprehensive vision of the mission of the church, the reason for which it was sent into the world, is captured by Michael Gorman in his assertion that "already in the first century the apostle Paul wanted the communities he addressed not merely to *believe* the gospel but to *become* the gospel, and in so doing to participate in the very life and mission of God."[7] From this perspective, the gospel is both a message to be proclaimed and a demonstration of how to live it out. The message, the good news, is that in Jesus Christ, God is liberating the world from the powers of sin and death and

5. Lesslie Newbigin, *The Open Secret: An Introduction to the Theology of Mission*, rev. ed. (Grand Rapids: Eerdmans, 1995), 48.

6. Newbigin, *Open Secret*, 48–49.

7. Michael J. Gorman, *Becoming the Gospel: Paul, Participation, and Mission*, The Gospel and Our Culture Series (Grand Rapids: Eerdmans, 2015), 2.

reconciling human beings with God, each other, and the whole of creation in order to establish shalom in the cosmos. The gospel demonstrates a way of life that provisionally announces that reality in the present even as it anticipates its coming eschatological fullness.

The church is the gathered community of the followers of Jesus Christ who believe in this good news and are prepared to live by it. In the words of David Bosch, mission is the participation of the church in the mission of God made known in Jesus Christ: it is "the good news of God's love, incarnated in the witness of a community, for the sake of the world."[8] We will now turn our attention to this aspect of incarnating the love of God in the witness of a community.

The Church as Community

In order to appreciate the concept of community, it is important to understand something of the ongoing conversation between individualist and communitarian traditions. It has become commonplace to think of Western culture as the heir of two traditions of thought that bear distinct sets of values that can shape the relationships between persons in society.

The *individualist* tradition asserts the primacy of the individual human person in all forms of social life and views the contract between individuals as the basis of all social interaction. This tradition promotes such values as personal freedom, self-improvement, privacy, achievement, independence, detachment, and self-interest. Although exercising these values may bring a person into contact with others, the essential meaning of such values is not connected to interaction among persons but to the rights and needs of individuals separate from their relationships with others.

At the heart of this tradition is *ontological individualism*, the belief that the ultimate truth of the human condition is not to be

8. Bosch, *Transforming Mission*, 532.

found in our societies or the relations we share with others but rather in our isolated individual selves. The individualist tradition is closely connected to liberal political theory. In this conception, the political order is based on social atomism together with the idea of the social contract. According to this theory, autonomous selves come together to form the state, contracting with each other to give up certain individual prerogatives to the whole for the sake of personal advantage.

The individualist tradition has its roots in seventeenth- and eighteenth-century thinkers who sought to cope intellectually with two cultural shifts underway in their era: the demise of the rigid status systems endemic to the older feudal society, and the rise of the modern world characterized by a market economy, industrialization, specialization, and urbanization. The emerging understanding looked to the contract between free persons, rather than to custom or tradition, as the basis for all human interactions. The architects of this view maintained that social rules, economic structures, and even the forming of family were artificial, convenient arrangements derived from contracts between individuals who were unable to attain personal identity and self-consciousness without them. In this context individual rights rather than responsibilities became the more basic moral concept.

Individualism continues to be a powerful influence in contemporary American society with its assumption of the autonomous self that exists independently of any tradition or community. This is evident in, for example, people's tendency to define themselves primarily through reference to particular choices they make. From this perspective, the autonomous self is viewed as the primary context in which the social and political structures of American culture take shape.

As an alternative to the individualist tradition, the *communitarian* tradition emphasizes the social nature of human existence. It maintains that our understanding of the self is formed by connections with other people, institutions, and traditions.

Thus, the tradition holds to the primacy of the group, elevates the importance of relationships for personal existence, and suggests that interaction among people takes on meaning only within the social context in which it occurs. It values relational qualities such as fellowship, belonging, dependence, social involvement, and the public good. Further, its advocates maintain that conceptions of what is right and proposals concerning the organization of society always presuppose some vision of the common good.

From the communitarian perspective, the fundamental short-coming of individualism is its minimization of the social dimension of life and its importance in the shaping of the self. With its focus on the autonomous self, individualism suggests that the process of discovering who we are and discerning our deepest convictions comes primarily through intense self-examination and, further-more, that this rigorous self-examination is best engaged in apart from the social traditions and communities in which we participate. Communitarians disagree; they assert that one can more success-fully develop these insights in relation to other people, institutions, and traditions, because we come to know ourselves through our interaction with others and our activity in relationships, groups, associations, and communities shaped by institutional structures and cultural patterns. Simply put, we are not ends in ourselves.

Communitarians emphasize the notion of the social self and the importance of the social unit for crucial aspects of human existence. For instance, communitarians maintain that the com-munities we participate in are integral to the ways in which we come to understand notions of truth, meaning, and values. They argue that we can no longer hold to the individualist paradigm that focuses on the self-reflective, autonomous subject, since the knowing process is dependent on a cognitive framework mediated to the individual by the community. This critique forms the basis for the replacement of the individualistic rationalism common in modernity with an understanding of knowledge and belief as socially and relationally constituted.

While the debate between these two traditions continues, some have questioned the value of opposing labels and suggested that the ideas are not sufficiently distinct to be of real value, particularly since neither tradition discounts the importance of the other. Hence, most contemporary individualists acknowledge the importance of community in the development of the self, while communitarians value aspects that are accented in the individualist tradition, such as the importance of independent judgment and honest self-expression as well as the significance of difference and diversity in healthy communities. The two ideas are interdependent. Human experience is always, simultaneously and inextricably, both social and individual. There is no identity formation apart from the social communities in which individuals participate, and there is no community apart from the individuals who make up the community. From a Christian theological perspective, human beings are individuals created for community.

Attempts to define *community* must take into account that people often participate in several communities simultaneously, and so notions of boundaries are fluid, overlapping, and interrelated. In addition, theorists differ about the nature of the term; there is no uniform conception. In spite of these challenges, the widespread use of the term and the ideas it connotes, coupled with the traction it has gained in contemporary thought, suggest that the notion of community remains very fruitful, particularly in light of the relational character of God and the significance of the idea in the biblical narratives. Hence, let us consider three central elements that can help shape the idea of the church as an integrated community rather than merely a collection of individuals.

First, a community consists of a group of people who are conscious that they share a similar frame of reference. Participants in a particular community, while they may have very different perspectives on a wide range of subjects and issues, also tend to share a similar outlook toward life. They are inclined to view the world in a similar manner, to examine and construe the world in a common fashion. This commonality often grows deeper the longer a person participates in a particular community as the group's particular outlook starts to function in a taken-for-granted fashion. This occurs as participants construct the world they inhabit using similar linguistic and symbolic tools and concepts, even if they do not all agree about the meaning of their world-constructing symbols.

Second, a sense of group focus appears to be present in all communities. This aspect is perhaps the most common in the various definitions of community. A community consists of a group of people who are socially connected and share in conversation and decision making in matters of communal concern as well as sharing common practices that both define and nurture the community. This focus on the group produces a shared sense of identity among the members of the community whose attention is directed toward the group and its significance in their lives. One important aspect of this group identity is the belief that as participants in the community, they engage in a common task that engenders a sense of solidarity among the members of the community. However, the group focus does not demand unanimity and uniformity of opinion; rather, what is indicative of community is a shared interest in participating in ongoing discussion as to what constitutes the identity of the group. A healthy community will be shaped by robust conversation, and even serious debate, concerning the group's commitments and ongoing concerns as it formulates vision and wrestles with the challenges of a changing world.

Finally, the group orientation of a community leads members to draw a sense of personal identity from the community. In this context, the group is a crucial factor in forming the identity of its members. Members of a community do not merely share a generally common outlook on life and the world, and they are not simply shaped by a group focus; they also understand their identity as being defined to some extent by the community of which they are a part. That is to say, the community becomes constitutive of their personal identity.

It is part of the mission of the church to establish communities that faithfully participate in the mission of God. This presents a challenge in the wake of the individualist tradition, which still shapes the intuitions and habits of contemporary culture. The individualism and social atomism that shape modern conceptions of the social order view society as the product of autonomous individuals who enter into a social contract that is personally advantageous. The ecclesiological outworking of this contractual conception sees the church as the voluntary association of individual believers whose identity precedes their presence in the congregation, in that their identity is supposedly constituted prior to their joining together to form the church. In this model the church is constituted by its members, rather than constituting them. The members of the church are deemed to be complete Christian individuals prior to and apart from their membership in the church. The church, in turn, is an aggregate of the individual Christians who contract with each other to form a Christian society.

This contractual view of ecclesiology continues to typify much contemporary church life. In North America, people often see religion as an individual choice that takes place prior to any communal or organizational commitment. In this context, engagement in a local congregation becomes simply participation in another voluntary society that often has a minimal role in identity formation. In addition, while participation in a visible church community traditionally has been considered an essential component of Christian faith, from a contractual viewpoint it is deemed optional.

Contractual political theory has played an undeniably beneficial role in the development of Western democracy, but its link to modern individualism has had devastating effects on ecclesiology and full communal participation in the mission of God. Contractual ecclesiology followed the development of Western democracy and, under the impulse of individualism, tends to devalue the church, reducing the community of Christ's disciples to little more than a particular lifestyle enclave, a society formed by persons united by their shared interest in certain religious practices or who believe that membership in a Christian group will contribute to their individual good. For this reason, the establishment of community in the church has become a pressing challenge and concern in contemporary ecclesiology. If the church is to truly and faithfully participate in the mission of God, the recovery of a genuine sense of community is crucial.

The Church: Image of God and Sign of the Kingdom

Christian theologians have traditionally constructed theological anthropology around the concept of the *imago Dei*. From the Judeo-Christian perspective, human identity is bound up with the idea that human beings are created in the image of God and therefore are bearers of the divine image. While the biblical writings assert that human beings are created in the image of God, they do not provide a detailed account of the precise meaning of this commitment. Theologians have offered various formulations through the years concerning the best way to understand the nature or content of the *imago Dei*.

Perhaps the most long-standing interpretation of the image sees it as a structure of the human person. In this understanding, the divine image consists of the properties that constitute human beings as human, with special emphasis placed on the capacity for rationality coupled with our moral nature. This view is widespread in the writings of the earliest Christians as well as among the medieval scholastic theologians. It was challenged to some extent in the Protestant Reformation, but it regained ascendancy in Protestant orthodox theology and continues to be influential in faith traditions influenced by scholastic thought.

Two concepts have moved the discussion forward: relationality and destiny. Long part of the Christian tradition, *relationality* received new emphasis in the work of the Protestant Reformers, who tended to place primary focus on the special standing before God that characterizes human existence rather than on a formal structure supposedly found within the human person. While this relationship was tarnished by human sin and rebellion, it is restored through Christ. The Reformers also extended the notion that the image of God is linked to human destiny. The groundwork for this idea was laid in the christological formulations of Irenaeus and his suggestion that Jesus is the "recapitulation" of the human story. Building on this idea, Martin Luther declared that although through sin humankind lost the image of God, it could be restored "through the Word and the Holy Spirit."[9] This restoration, which begins in the present, reaches its climax in the eschatological consummation of all things and raises humans to a stature that is even higher than what was lost in the fall. The perfection of the divine image is the eternal life for which human beings were created. Hence, in this sense the *imago Dei* is ultimately God's intention and goal, or *destiny*, for human beings.

From this perspective, the creation of human beings in the image of God is an ontological status, a relational and vocational calling, and a destiny toward which human beings are moving. This eschatological destination is also a future reality that is present now in the form of human potential. As Daniel Migliore states, "Being created in the image of God is not a state or condition but a movement with a goal: human beings are restless for a fulfillment of life not yet realized."[10] Genesis 1:26 connects this fulfillment with the concept of dominion: "Then God said, 'Let us make humankind in our image, according to our likeness; and let them have dominion over the fish of the sea, and over the birds of the air, and over the cattle, and over all the wild animals of the earth, and over every creeping thing that creeps upon the earth.'"

9. Martin Luther, *Lectures on Genesis*, in *Luther's Works*, ed. Jaroslav Pelikan, trans. George V. Schick, American Edition (St. Louis: Concordia, 1958), 2:141.

10. Daniel L. Migliore, *Faith Seeking Understanding: An Introduction to Christian Theology* (Grand Rapids: Eerdmans, 1991), 128.

Rather than reading dominion against the background of the ideology of modern industrial society, however, we must place the concept within the context of the royal theology of the Hebrew Bible. The kings of the ancient Near East often left images of themselves in cities or territories where they could not be present in person. Just as earthly kings erected images of themselves to indicate their dominion over territory where they were not physically present, so human beings are placed upon the earth in God's image as God's sovereign emblem or image to represent God's dominion on the earth.[11] Human beings are called to reflect God's loving care of creation.

Viewing the image of God as connected to our divinely given calling to represent God means that all persons are made in God's image and that all share in the one human *telos*. However, the New Testament writers apply the concept of the divine image particularly to Jesus Christ (2 Cor. 4:4–6; Col. 1:15), who is the clear representation of the character of God. By extension, those who are united to Christ share in his role as the image of God. All who are "in Christ" are being transformed into the image of Christ so that their lives may reflect his glory: "And all of us, with unveiled faces, seeing the glory of the Lord as though reflected in a mirror, are being transformed into the same image from one degree of glory to another; for this comes from the Lord, the Spirit" (2 Cor. 3:18). In fact, it is to conformity to Christ as the likeness of God that God has destined humanity (Rom. 8:29; 1 John 3:2). For this reason, Paul proclaims the hope that we will bear the image of God in Christ through our participation in Christ's resurrection (1 Cor. 15:49–53). In short, the entire biblical panorama may be read as presenting the purpose of God as bringing into being a people who reflect the divine character and thus fulfill the vocational calling to be the image of God.

11. Gerhard von Rad, *Genesis*, trans. John H. Marks, Old Testament Library (Philadelphia: Westminster, 1972), 58.

In Matthew's Gospel we read that after the arrest of John, Jesus withdrew to Galilee to fulfill what had been spoken by Isaiah. Then Matthew tells us: "From that time Jesus began to proclaim, 'Repent, for the kingdom of heaven has come near'" (Matt. 4:17). Similarly, Mark says that the beginning of the gospel coincides with the preaching of Jesus in Galilee: "The time is fulfilled, and the kingdom of God has come near; repent, and believe in the good news" (Mark 1:15). With this announcement, the Gospel writers are declaring that after long and often difficult years of anticipating the reign of God in the world, in Jesus of Nazareth God's kingdom has come near in a new and decisive way that calls for action among those who have eyes to see and ears to hear. "If the New Testament spoke only of the proclamation of the kingdom there could be nothing to justify the adjective 'new.' The prophets and John the Baptist also proclaimed the kingdom. What is new is that in Jesus the kingdom is present."[12] For those whose thought was shaped by the Hebrew Bible, the inference is clear: the coming of the kingdom of God is no longer a distant, far-off hope but a present reality in the person of Jesus. The proclamation and presence of the kingdom of God in the person of Jesus calls forth the action of repentance, a turning from the ways of sin and death, from the selfish exploitation and oppression of others. It is a call to a new way of life that is expressed as discipleship.

The church is sent into the world after the pattern by which the Father sent the Son. The church is to be a sign of the kingdom of God through its proclamation of the gospel in word and deed, and as a community of persons who are committed both to practicing discipleship in the way of Jesus and to making disciples in keeping with Jesus's last instructions to his followers in Matthew 28:18–20: "And Jesus came and said to them, 'All authority in heaven and on earth has been given to me. Go therefore and make disciples of all nations, baptizing them in the name of the Father and of

12. Newbigin, *Open Secret*, 40.

the Son and of the Holy Spirit, and teaching them to obey everything that I have commanded you. And remember, I am with you
always, to the end of the age.'" As we saw in the previous chapter,
discipleship is God's plan for changing the world in keeping with
the divine mission.

As the church follows the pattern of Jesus, proclaiming the
gospel of the kingdom and God's love for all people and calling
on those who hear this good news to repent of sin and become
disciples of Jesus, a new way of life in the world is envisioned and
established. This leads to the formation of a new community, a
welcoming and inclusive community that lives the love of God for
the world and transcends the divisions that are so often used to
exclude people from the blessing and peace of God's kingdom. As
the church pursues and embodies this inclusive vision of new community through gospel proclamation and discipleship in the way
of Jesus, it bears the image of God as a sign of God's kingdom.

The Church: Body of Christ and Instrument of the Kingdom

As the body of Christ, the church is sent into the world and called
to continue the mission of Jesus in the power of the Spirit. While
it certainly is true that God is at work outside the church, the New
Testament characterization of the church as the body of Christ
leads to the conclusion that it is intended to be a focal point of the
mission of God in the world. The mission of the church is shaped
by the mission and ministry of Jesus. Two biblical texts from the
Gospel of Luke, among many that could be cited, point to the
mission of Jesus and should characterize the life and witness of
the church sent by God into the world after the fashion in which
Jesus was sent.

The first is found in Luke's account of the inaugural events of
Jesus's public ministry. The stage has been set: Mary has been
told by the angel Gabriel that, though she is a virgin, she will give
birth to a son to be named Jesus, and he will be Son of the Most

High whose kingdom will never end. At this Mary rejoices in the Lord who has brought down the proud and powerful and lifted up the lowly, filling the hungry with good things and sending the rich away empty. The angel of the Lord has announced the birth of the Messiah to shepherds with the promise that this is good news of great joy for all people. John the Baptist has prepared the way by proclaiming the way of the Lord, and Jesus has endured the temptations of the devil in the wilderness.

Then Jesus begins speaking and teaching in the Galilean synagogues and finally comes to Nazareth, where he had been raised. There he proclaims the words of the prophet Isaiah as a summary of the work he has been sent to accomplish:

> When he came to Nazareth, where he had been brought up, he went to the synagogue on the Sabbath day, as was his custom. He stood up to read, and the scroll of the prophet Isaiah was given to him. He unrolled the scroll and found the place where it was written: "The Spirit of the Lord is upon me, because he has anointed me to bring good news to the poor. He has sent me to proclaim release to the captives and recovery of sight to the blind, to let the oppressed go free, to proclaim the year of the Lord's favor." And he rolled up the scroll, gave it back to the attendant, and sat down. The eyes of all in the synagogue were fixed on him. Then he began to say to them, "Today this scripture has been fulfilled in your hearing." (Luke 4:16–21)

Here at the beginning of his public ministry, Jesus sets forth a central component of his mission to turn the world around and put it the way God intended it to be. This component can be summarized in one word: liberation. This emphasis on the liberating ministry of Jesus points to an understanding of the church as the community of Christ's followers who join with Jesus in his struggle to liberate humanity from the forces of oppression and enslavement. The mission of the church, in keeping with the mission of Jesus, is to proclaim and live out the meaning of God's

liberating activity so that those who live under the oppressive powers of this world will see that their liberation from these powers
constitutes the mission of God in the world. The church, as the
body of Christ, is the instrument of God in this liberating activity
of social justice for all.

This concern for the poor and marginalized is powerfully expressed in Matthew 25:31–40 and Jesus's story about separating
the sheep and the goats:

> When the Son of Man comes in his glory, and all the angels with
> him, then he will sit on the throne of his glory. All the nations
> will be gathered before him, and he will separate people one from
> another as a shepherd separates the sheep from the goats, and he
> will put the sheep at his right hand and the goats at the left. Then
> the king will say to those at his right hand, "Come, you that are
> blessed by my Father, inherit the kingdom prepared for you from
> the foundation of the world; for I was hungry and you gave me
> food, I was thirsty and you gave me something to drink, I was
> a stranger and you welcomed me, I was naked and you gave me
> clothing, I was sick and you took care of me, I was in prison and
> you visited me." Then the righteous will answer him, "Lord, when
> was it that we saw you hungry and gave you food, or thirsty and
> gave you something to drink? And when was it that we saw you a
> stranger and welcomed you, or naked and gave you clothing? And
> when was it that we saw you sick or in prison and visited you?"
> And the king will answer them, "Truly I tell you, just as you did
> it to one of the least of these who are members of my family, you
> did it to me."

Likewise, in James 1:27: "Religion that is pure and undefiled before
God, the Father, is this: to care for orphans and widows in their
distress, and to keep oneself unstained by the world."

These texts point to the calling of the church to participate in
the temporal, here-and-now activity of liberation. The concrete-
ness of these texts points beyond common interpretations that

imagine the activity of liberation primarily, or only, in a spiritual sense. Indeed, it has been one of the great misunderstandings of the mission of Jesus in the history of Christianity that he was preaching only a spiritual kingdom, primarily concerned with the destiny of individuals in the next life. That notion has had pernicious effects in the life of the church and the social contexts in which it has been in a dominant cultural position. It has been used to justify the maintenance of the status quo in which the poor and marginalized are ignored and oppressed, while claiming divine sanction for their plight and pandering to the rich and powerful.

Embedded in the Hebrew tradition, the call to liberation is to be enacted in the present in such a way that the existing social order will actually change. Liberation theologian Gustavo Gutiérrez speaks of liberation in three senses—political, cultural, and spiritual—all of which are part of the mission of the church. While these are interrelated, they are not the same; none is present without the others, but they remain distinct. Together they are part of a single, all-encompassing salvific process that takes root in temporal political history but is not exhausted by it. As Gutiérrez writes, "We can say that the historical, political liberating event *is* the growth of the Kingdom and *is* a salvific event; but it is not *the* coming of the Kingdom, not *all* of salvation."[13] As the body of Christ in the world, the church participates in this historical process as an instrument of the kingdom of God in accordance with the mission of God and the good news of the gospel.

The extent of liberation and its challenges are graphically illustrated in what occurs immediately after Jesus concludes his proclamation in the synagogue. We're told that those present "got up, drove him out of the town, and led him to the brow of the hill on which their town was built, so that they might hurl him off the cliff" (Luke 4:29). Why?

13. Gustavo Gutiérrez, *Theology of Liberation* (Maryknoll, NY: Orbis, 1973), 176–77.

Jesus has been making the point that liberation extends to all people, not just to a particular group. To make this point he tells the stories of the great prophets Elijah and Elisha. Elijah was sent to help a widow, but not a Jewish one. Elisha healed a leper who also happened to be the commander of the enemy army. The liberating grace and love of God are for all, not just the chosen few. This is not what the crowd wanted to hear—they were waiting for God to liberate Israel from pagan enemies by bringing condemnation and wrath on their oppressors. Instead, Jesus implies that Israel's enemies are also the intended beneficiaries of the good news of God's love for all people.

This is the scandal of God's love. It extends to all people— ourselves and our enemies, whoever they may be. We rejoice that God loves us and offers us the grace of forgiveness and liberation in our lives. But we must never forget that along with this gift, we receive the responsibility to extend it to others, even at cost to ourselves. This is the message of Christian faith: that while we were enemies of God, God loved us in Jesus Christ. In gratitude and thanksgiving, the church is called to share the liberating news of God's love with everyone.

A second text, in addition to Luke 4, that points to the mission of Jesus is Luke 19:1–10, the story of Jesus and Zacchaeus the tax collector, which concludes with Jesus saying to Zacchaeus: "Today salvation has come to this house, because he too is a son of Abraham. For the Son of Man came to seek out and to save the lost" (vv. 9–10). The church has been sent into the world after the pattern of Jesus to seek the lost and to proclaim the good news of salvation in Christ. Evangelism is a central aspect of the reconciling mission of God to a lost and broken world.

In response to those who have separated evangelism from the pursuit of social justice and liberation, note the comment of Zacchaeus in the preceding verse: "Look, half of my possessions, Lord, I will give to the poor; and if I have defrauded anyone of anything, I will pay back four times as much" (v. 8). The response of Zacchaeus to Jesus, which includes repentance, reformation, and restoration, leads to the kind of individual transformation that has a direct effect on the social order. Evangelism and social justice are inseparable elements of the proclamation of the good news that in Jesus Christ, God is reconciling all things.

The Church: Dwelling Place of the Spirit and Foretaste of the Kingdom

The Spirit is given to the church to empower it for participation in God's mission to establish a new community that transcends the divisions that so easily divide and cause hostility and suspicion among human beings made in God's image. In the New Testament this vision of a new, inclusive community is particularly focused on the inclusion of the gentiles in the family of God. In the contemporary setting this vision includes those of every tribe and nation. As the church engages in this aspect of mission, it lives into its calling to be a provisional demonstration of God's intentions for all people and, as such, a foretaste of the kingdom of God.

One of the ways in which the church participates with the Spirit in this work is through telling and enacting stories that forge links between past and present traditions and the future. The church is a community with a narrative that begins in the calling of God to be a blessing to the world, the life and teachings of Jesus, and his commission to make disciples of the nations in keeping with the intentions of the kingdom of God. In an important sense, that church is constituted by that narrative that begins in the past and extends into the future.

This constitutive narrative does not view time merely as a continuous flow of generally meaningless events and occurrences but rather as a story in which the church interprets the present with a sense of transcendent purpose and thereby presents time as a meaningful whole. This founding narrative begins with the paradigmatic event(s) that called the church into being. The stories of

beginnings and crucial milestones that mark its subsequent trajectory are told and enacted again and again. More important than
merely articulating past events, recalling the narrative retrieves
the constitutive past for the sake of personal and communal life
in the present. Or put another way, reciting the constitutive narrative of the past places particular churches within the narrative
that constituted the emergence of the universal church. These
actions retrieve the past, bringing it into the present, and thereby
reconstitute the church in the present as the contemporary embodiment of a communal tradition that spans the years.

This history does not end in the past or the present. It extends
into the future and anticipates continuous development, moving
forward toward an ideal that has not yet been realized. Churches
expectantly look forward to the time when the community's purpose and goals will be fully actualized. This expectation serves as
an ongoing admonition to its members to embody the communal
vision in the present.

In keeping this vision before its members, a community acts
as a community of hope. The constitutive narrative of the community stretches from the ancient past to the future and provides
a vantage point for life in the present. It also offers a plausible
explanation of present existence, for it provides the overarching
theme through which members of the community can view their
lives and the present moment in history as a part of a story that
transcends the present. In this manner, as the community retells its
constitutive narrative, it functions as an interpretive community.

The telling of the constitutive narrative contained in the Bible
is accompanied by and accentuated through sacred practices and
rituals that bring the community together. These rituals or sacra-
ments of baptism, communion, liturgy, and the preaching and
teaching of Scripture are essential elements of the mission of the
church. They increase the solidarity of members and strengthen
their commitments. These practices of commitment and solidarity
define the community's way of life and shape patterns of identity

and obligation that serve to keep the community vibrant and alert to new growth opportunities that are in continuity with its past.

While in one sense the contemporary Western church has struggled to manifest true community, in another sense the church is a community through the work of the Spirit. The church is the fellowship of those persons who gather around the narrative of God at work in the world according to the witness of the Bible. What is important to remember is that the God of this narrative is the One who constitutes the church.

More specifically, the church is formed by the work of the Spirit speaking through Scripture for the purpose of world creation. This is a social, communal world in accordance with the nature of God as social. By speaking through Scripture, centered as it is on the narrative of God acting on our behalf to fashion a new creation, the Spirit brings into being a new community, a fellowship of persons who gather around the name of Jesus Christ. Hence, the church is more than the aggregate of its members. It is a particular people shaped by a particular "constitutive narrative"—namely, the Spirit-appropriated, community-fashioning narrative of Scripture that spans the ages stretching from creation to consummation. As the church retells this constitutive narrative, it functions as a community of memory and hope and provides an interpretive framework through which its members find meaning in their personal and communal stories. Through the Spirit, participation in the life of the church links the present with the full scope of God's action in history, which spans the ages from the "beginning" (Gen. 1:1) to the "end" with the consummation of the ages and the establishment of "a new heaven and a new earth" (Rev. 21:1).

As a consequence of this shared narrative, Christians are in solidarity with each other around the globe and throughout history. In the local church, this solidarity works its way out in the practical dimensions of fellowship, support, and nurture that its members discover through their relationships with each other as a communal people. And in this process, the church becomes an alternative community for the common good. In short, as James McClendon succinctly states, the church is a community "understood not as privileged access to God or to sacred status, but as sharing together in a storied life of obedient service to and with Christ."[14]

A central feature of this new community gathered together in the name of Jesus is corporate worship. In the worship of God, the community comes together as one body and declares its adoration of God, its dependence on God for its witness in the world, and its thankfulness for the gifts of faith, hope, and love. It also enacts the story of God's mission in the world and its participation in that mission through shared liturgy. In this way, worship is a central element of the witness of the church to the reign of God in the world. As the church gathers together in worship, we celebrate God's presence, enact God's mission, share concerns, pray, and seek the strength to continue on in faithful witness.

As such, worship is a fundamental expression of the mission of the church, not an activity separate from that mission. It is a part of the comprehensive calling for which the church has been sent into the world: to bear witness in thought, word, and deed to the love of God for the world. In this way, the church is a foretaste of the vision from Revelation 7:9–10 in which "a great multitude that no one could count, from every nation, from all tribes and peoples and languages" stands before God and gives thanks in worship and praise for the salvation of God in Jesus Christ. Through a new life together of interdependent relationality and corporate worship, the church bears witness to a new world that finds its coherence in the love of God revealed in Jesus Christ and attested by the power of the Spirit.

This life together is a foretaste of the world as it is willed to be by God. However, the world as God wills it to be is not a present

---

14. James William McClendon Jr., *Ethics: Systematic Theology* (Nashville: Abingdon, 1986), 1:28.

reality but rather lies in the eschatological future. Hence, Jesus taught his disciples to pray: "Our Father in heaven, hallowed be your name. Your kingdom come. Your will be done, on earth as it is in heaven" (Matt. 6:9–10). This is a prayer to bring into being a new reality when God will put everything right and order the cosmos in accordance with the intentions of creation. Because this future reality is God's determined will for creation—that which cannot be shaken (Heb. 12:26–28)—it is far more real, objective, and actual than the present world, which is even now passing away (1 Cor. 7:31). The church in the present is a foretaste of the manifestation of this future eschatological reality for which we live, work, hope, and pray and in which all of creation finds its connectedness in Jesus Christ (Col. 1:17).

While the elements of the mission of the church to be a sign, instrument, and foretaste of the kingdom of God can be distinguished, they cannot be separated. They are bound together in overlapping, interrelated ways. One particularly helpful example that brings the three together, though without using the same terminology, is the work of Raymond Fung, former secretary for evangelism in the World Council of Churches' Commission on World Mission and Evangelism.[15] He offers a strategy for evangelism that includes each of the elements we have discussed. He suggests that local Christian congregations, in partnership with other people, pursue the vision outlined in Isaiah 65:20–23:

> No more shall there be in it
>   an infant that lives but a few days,
>   or an old person who does not live out a lifetime;
> for one who dies at a hundred years will be considered a
>   youth,
>   and one who falls short of a hundred will be considered
>   accursed.

15. Raymond Fung, *The Isaiah Vision: An Ecumenical Strategy for Congregational Evangelism* (Geneva: WCC Publications, 1992).

They shall build houses and inhabit them;
    they shall plant vineyards and eat their fruit.
They shall not build and another inhabit;
    they shall not plant and another eat;
for like the days of a tree shall the days of my people be,
    and my chosen shall long enjoy the work of their
       hands.
They shall not labor in vain,
    or bear children for calamity;
for they shall be offspring blessed by the LORD—
    and their descendants as well.

In pursuing this vision in partnership with others, we declare to our neighbors that the "God we believe in is one who protects the children, empowers the elderly, and walks with working men and women. As Christians, we wish to act accordingly. We believe you share in similar concerns. Let us join hands." As the church works at this vision, we invite our partners to worship God with us. We say: Doing this work is hard. There are many needs and problems. Occasionally, we need to pause, share concerns, pray, and seek the strength to continue through worshiping our God. "Would you join us? You would be most welcome."[16] In the process of working toward the Isaiah vision, the partners will grow to know and understand each other as trust and friendship develop and we become comfortable with each other. In this context, occasions will emerge when it is appropriate to invite partners to become disciples of Jesus. "Whether you are somebody or nobody, rich or poor, powerful or powerless, you are invited to enter into friendship with Jesus and fellowship with the church. You are called to turn around. Take up your cross and follow Jesus, together with us. We are ordinary people called to do extraordinary things with God."[17] In this model the church is a sign of the kingdom in mak-

16. Fung, *Isaiah Vision*, 2.
17. Fung, *Isaiah Vision*, 3.

ing disciples, an instrument of the kingdom in working for a better world for those who are vulnerable and those who labor, and a foretaste of the kingdom in worship and life together.

Mission after Christendom

Before turning our attention to the profile and practice of missional theology, it is important to consider briefly the effects of Christendom as it relates to the church and its sense of mission. Tragically, the church has often not lived up to the missional calling we have just described. The missionary expansion of the church has frequently been an exercise in the extension of empire through the process of colonization and has used the Bible as a justification for this activity, beginning with the establishment of the church in the Roman Empire. Rome did not make Christianity its official religion to enable the church to critique and challenge its practices and assumptions concerning the use and manifestation of power. This had particular consequences for the interpretation of Scripture. While all of the texts that would eventually make up the Christian canon were produced at the margins of the Roman Empire, the complicity that arose between Christianity and Rome in the advent of Christendom meant that the margins moved to the center and were interpreted accordingly. "Locked in the crushing embrace of the Vulgate, the first official Bible of imperial Christianity, the primary function of the biblical texts became that of legitimizing the imperial status quo, a function that, covertly when not overtly, continued into the modern period."[18]

As missiologists reflected on the missionary expansion of the church over the last two centuries, many began to be concerned about the particular shape of this missionary enterprise. It has become increasingly clear that Western mission has traditionally

18. Stephen D. Moore, "Paul after Empire," in *The Colonized Apostle: Paul through Postcolonial Eyes*, ed. Christopher D. Stanley (Minneapolis: Fortress, 2011), 22.

been very much an Anglo-European church centered enterprise
and that the gospel has been passed on in the cultural shape of the
Western church. While this approach contributed to the growth
of the church throughout the world, it also presents a challenge in
that the formation and structures of the Western church are not
missional but rather have been formed and shaped in the context
of a historical and social setting which for centuries considered
itself officially Christian.

In this context the church was intimately involved in shaping
the religious and cultural life of Western society. This situation
led to what is known as Christendom, a system of church-state
partnership and cultural hegemony in which the Christian religion
maintains a unique, privileged, and protected place in society,
and the Christian church is its legally and socially established
institutional form. This model of the church, and the outlooks
and intuitions that attend to it, are so deeply pervasive that even
when the formal and legal structures of Christendom are removed,
as in the case of North America, its legacy is perpetuated in the
traditions, structures, and attitudes that are its entailments. The
continuance of the intuitions and entailments of Christendom,
even in the aftermath of its formal demise, is known as functional
Christendom. In this context, the church continues to maintain
patterns of life and witness that are consistent with the traditions
shaped by its establishment past, although it no longer occupies
this position in society.

From the perspective of Christendom that characterized the
established church in the West, "mission became only one of the
many programs of the church. Mission boards emerged in Western churches to do the work of foreign mission. Yet even here the
Western churches understood themselves as sending churches, and
they assumed the destination of their sending to be the pagan
reaches of the world."[19] It was assumed that these distant realms

19. Guder, *Missional Church*, 6.

would benefit from the influence of Western culture as well as the gospel. In a similar manner, many churches developed home mission programs and strategies in order to confront and attempt to hold at bay the emerging secularism of society that threatened to undermine the legacy Christian culture. These programs often involved significant political activism as an important part of preserving the ethos of a Christian society.

This desire to preserve and spread not only the gospel but also the particular ethos and culture of Western Christendom connected Christian mission with colonialism and colonization in the name of the gospel of Jesus Christ. This has had disastrous consequences for the practice of mission. Richard Twiss, a member of the Rosebud Lakota Tribe, comments: "Christian mission among the tribes of North America has not been very good news. What worldview influences allowed the Creator's story of creation and redemption to morph into a hegemonic colonial myth justifying the genocide and exploitation of America's First Nations people?"[20] Speaking of his own experience, he explains the pressure imposed by white Christians to regard the music, dance, drumming, and ceremony of his Lakota culture as "unclean" and inappropriate for followers of Jesus. The implicit message was that the old and familiar rituals and experiences had passed away and all things had "become white." "This meant I needed to leave my Indian ways behind me, because I had a new identity in Christ, and it WAS NOT Indian! The Bible was used to demonize just about everything important to our cultural sense of being one with God and creation."[21] This social and cultural colonization in the name of Christianity has had devastating consequences and has been all too typical of the interaction between Western mission

---

20. Richard Twiss, "Living in Transition, Embracing Community, and Envisioning God's Mission as Trinitarian Mutuality: Reflections from a Native-American Follower of Jesus," in *Remembering Jamestown: Hard Questions about Christian Mission*, ed. Amos Yong and Barbara Brown Zikmund (Eugene, OR: Pickwick, 2010), 93.

21. Twiss, "Living in Transition," 94.

and the indigenous cultures it has encountered. A particular set of social and cultural assumptions and presuppositions has stamped the Bible and theology in its image, in this case that of Western culture, and then this has been imposed on another group of people in the name of God and truth.

When this occurs, the voices of those who do not participate in the assumptions and presuppositions of the majority are marginalized or eclipsed, often under the guise of claims that they are not being faithful to Scripture or the Christian tradition. Christian mission that would bear faithful witness to the gospel of Jesus Christ must resist and repudiate this colonizing trajectory. In light of the church's history and complicity with the forces of colonization, the mission and witness of the church must be reimagined in keeping with the principles and values of the kingdom proclaimed by Jesus. Missional theology seeks to reimagine Christian witness so that it more faithfully reflects the mission of God and the participation of the church in that mission.

CHAPTER

3

Missional Theology

In the previous chapter I cited a statement from the influential book *Missional Church* concerning the future of North American congregations: "Either we are defined by mission, or we reduce the scope of the gospel and the mandate of the church. Thus our challenge today is to move from church with mission to missional church."[1] The move from church with mission to missional church has significant implications for the practice of theology.

As with the church, the impulses and assumptions that have shaped the discipline of theology in the West are those of Christendom rather than the mission of God. Theology is still often taught and discussed from the vantage point of early modern debates and concerns, with little reference to the missional character of God and the corresponding missional vocation of the church. Courses in missions or missiology are generally taught only in the practical theology department and, apart from a generic introductory

1. Darrell L. Guder, ed., *Missional Church: A Theological Vision for the Sending of the Church in North America* (Grand Rapids: Eerdmans, 1998), 6.

course, are often thought to be primarily for those planning to participate in cross-cultural ministries. Rarely are such courses taught in the systematics department, and the disciplines of missiology and systematic theology have generally evidenced little significant overlap and cross-fertilization. Some signs exist that this is beginning to change, but progress is slow. Generally speaking, most teaching and research in Western universities and schools of theology remains in thrall to traditional academic models that stress detached objectivity in the study of any discipline, including theology.

Such an outlook is antithetical to the practice of Christian theology, particularly in light of its missional dimension. As Andrew Kirk remarks, theology that seeks to bear faithful witness to the living God "must have a personal dimension oriented to the present: that is, to personal, openly declared preferences involving engagement and commitment, including a solid identification with the Christian community." The reason for this, he notes, is that the subject of theology, the living God, makes demands, sets tasks, and calls us to obedience. In this context, the study of theology cannot remain detached and uncommitted.[2] If theology is to serve the life of the church and its witness to the gospel, and if we assume that "the church can exist as truly itself only when dedicated to the mission of God, a burning question ensues: How should one reinvent theology and theological education so that they flow naturally for an integral perspective on God's consistent will and activity in the world?"[3]

Like the challenge facing the church in moving from church with mission to missional church, so the discipline of theology, if it is to serve the church and be faithful to its subject, must move from theology with a mission component to a truly missional conception of theology.

2. J. Andrew Kirk, *The Mission of Theology and Theology as Mission* (Valley Forge, PA: Trinity Press, 1997), 9–10.
3. Kirk, *Mission of Theology*, 2.

As noted at the outset of chapter 1, a missional approach to theology arises from the conviction that the triune God is, by God's very nature, a missionary God and that therefore the church of this God is missionary by its very nature.[4] The idea of mission is at the heart of the biblical narratives concerning the work of God in human history.[5] The missional call to the church is captured in the words of Jesus recorded in the Gospel of John: "As the Father has sent me, so I send you" (John 20:21). David Bosch observes that mission is derived from the very nature of God and must be situated in the context of the doctrine of the Trinity rather than ecclesiology or soteriology. In this context the logic of the classical doctrine of the *missio Dei* expressed as God the Father sending the Son, and the Father and the Son sending the Spirit, may be expanded to include another movement: "Father, Son, and Spirit sending the church into the world."[6] From this perspective, the church is seen as an instrument and witness of God's mission to the world, not its end. The various historical, cultural, global, and contemporary embodiments of the church may be viewed as a series of local iterations of God's universal mission of love to all of creation.

In summary, (1) the mission of God from all eternity is love; (2) creation is the result of the expansive nature of God's love, and God desires that all of creation come to participate in the fellowship of divine love; (3) God calls forth a community to participate in the divine mission as a sign, instrument, and foretaste of the kingdom of God and a witness to the good news of God's love for the world; and (4) this singular community is manifested in numerous local communities from every tribe and nation.

4. See John G. Flett, *The Witness of God: The Trinity, Missio Dei, Karl Barth and the Nature of Christian Community* (Grand Rapids: Eerdmans, 2010).

5. On the centrality of mission in Scripture, see Christopher J. H. Wright, *The Mission of God: Unlocking the Bible's Grand Narrative* (Downers Grove, IL: IVP Academic, 2006).

6. David Bosch, *Transforming Mission: Paradigm Shifts in Theology of Mission*, 20th anniv. ed. (Maryknoll, NY: Orbis, 2011), 399.

Figure 3.1
A triangular model of gospel-church-culture relationships

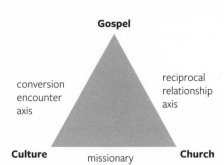

Source: George R. Hunsberger, "The Newbigin Gauntlet: Developing a Domestic Missiology for North America," in *The Church between Gospel and Culture: The Emerging Mission in North America* (Grand Rapids: Eerdmans, 1996), 9. Used with permission.

The manifestation of God's universal mission to creation in local communities draws culture into the forefront of missional theological conversation. Lesslie Newbigin provides an important interpretive framework for the development of a missional theology.[7] Missiologist George Hunsberger has provided a helpful summary of Newbigin's work on the interactions between gospel, church, and culture. He speaks of three axes that form what he calls the Newbigin triad: the gospel-culture axis as the conversion encounter; the gospel-church axis as the reciprocal relationship; and the church-culture axis as the missionary encounter (see fig. 3.1).[8]

7. Among the many writings of Lesslie Newbigin on these interactions, see particularly *Foolishness to the Greeks: The Gospel and Western Culture* (Grand Rapids: Eerdmans, 1998); *The Gospel in a Pluralist Society* (Grand Rapids: Eerdmans, 1989); and *The Open Secret: An Introduction to the Theology of Mission*, rev. ed. (Grand Rapids: Eerdmans, 1995).

8. George R. Hunsberger, "The Newbigin Gauntlet: Developing a Domestic Missiology for North America," in *The Church between Gospel and Culture: The Emerging Mission in North America* (Grand Rapids: Eerdmans, 1996), 3–25. See also George R. Hunsberger, *Bearing the Witness of the Spirit: Lesslie Newbigin's Theology of Cultural Plurality* (Grand Rapids: Eerdmans, 1998).

The gospel-culture axis affirms that all articulations of the gospel are culture specific. According to Newbigin, we must acknowledge that there is no such thing as a pure gospel unencumbered by the trappings of a particular culture. "The gospel always comes as the testimony of a community which, if it is faithful, is trying to live out the meaning of the gospel in a certain style of life, certain ways of holding property, of maintaining law and order, of carrying on production and consumption, and so on. Every interpretation of the gospel is embodied in some cultural form."[9] The gospel-church axis affirms that the understanding of the gospel of any particular community is shaped by the theological and ecclesial traditions of that community.

The church-culture axis affirms the plurality of the church as culturally distinct Christian communities that embody varying conceptions of the gospel in the midst of their particular social and historical circumstances. The inexhaustible fullness of the gospel is made manifest in the cultural expansion of the church as communities emerge and interact with one another. The process of contextualization is not something that takes place after the establishment of the biblical texts, their interpretations, and corresponding doctrines. Rather, it is fully present in all of these forms of witness and cannot be removed or eliminated. Contextuality is an inherent part of the process of understanding and communication. From this perspective, biblical interpretation, meaning, and communication always involve the recontextualization of texts and their particular appropriations in a variety of social and historical settings. This ongoing activity of recontextualization in and for a diversity of cultural settings is the essence of missional theology. It has an inherently relational dimension that involves understanding the social contexts of other interpreters as well as texts.

This relational dimension significantly reconfigures common notions of Christian witness with respect to the communication

9. Newbigin, *Gospel in a Pluralist Society*, 144.

of the gospel, particularly with respect to traditional forms of cross-cultural activity. In the intercultural model, witness does not consist in the delivery of pre-established conceptions of the gospel and Christian teaching, in which the recipients of the message are treated as the objects of the one proclaiming the message and also are expected to receive the message just as presented if they are to benefit from its promises. Such an approach leads to the message functioning like the introduction of an alien ideology that, if accepted, undermines and subverts the ecosystem of the existing culture and has detrimental effects on its participants. Rather, intercultural understanding involves genuine, loving concern for others and for the cultural settings that shape their identity. Applied to the task of theology, the discipline becomes an enterprise in mutual understanding in which all of the partners provide crucial and necessary elements to the discourse.

Following this model, Justo González conceives of the mission of the church as being shaped not only by the need of the world to hear the gospel but also by the need of the church to hear and listen to the world in all the diversity of its nations, cultures, and ethnicities. In this way the church will have a fuller understanding of the gospel as Christians from all the earth bring the richness of their experience to bear on its proclamation and witness. Hence, the church invites all the peoples and nations of the earth to the gospel not solely because they need the gospel "but also because the church needs the 'nations' in order to be fully 'catholic.' If 'catholic' means 'according to the whole,' as long as part of the whole remains outside, or is brought in without being allowed to speak from its own perspective, catholicity itself is truncated."[10]

The intercultural dialogue between these communities is vital to missional theology and builds resistance to inflexible dogmatism that would restrict the truth of the gospel, as well as to an

10. Justo González, *Out of Every Tribe and Nation: Christian Theology at the Ethnic Roundtable* (Nashville: Abingdon, 1992), 28–29.

"anything goes" relativism that could eclipse it. Framing the interactions between gospel, church, and culture in this way helps communities to resist the danger of excessive accommodation of the gospel message to culture—or, on the other hand, the danger of being viewed as entirely apart from culture.

Consequently, the work of theology must account for the social and cultural situatedness of all interpreters and interpretations, while also taking seriously the God who is the subject of theology. I will say more in the next chapter about the pluriform character of revelation; here I simply note that God is living and active rather than static. This means that God cannot be comprehended apart from God's actions and ongoing active relations. In the same way, the relationship of human beings to God is best conceived of in active rather than static terms. Relations with God are not something that can be possessed once and for all; rather, they are events that must be continually accounted for by the ongoing work and grace of God. In other words, the ultimate source of theology is the living God who, as a dynamic living being, is always in movement.

Reformed theologian Karl Barth has helpfully reflected on this aspect of theology as attempting to trace the movement of God. What the church is called to do is simply to follow attentively the movement of God. In doing so through word and deed, it is important to remember that the action is God's, not ours, and that our role in this following of the movement of God is always "an instant in a *movement*, and any view of it is comparable to the momentary view of a bird in flight. Aside from the movement it is absolutely meaningless, incomprehensible, and impossible." Therefore this movement is not of human origin and cannot be reduced to human comprehension; it is rather "a movement from above, a movement from a third dimension," by which Barth means "the movement of God in history or, otherwise expressed, the movement of God in consciousness, the movement whose power and import are revealed in the resurrection of Jesus Christ from the dead."[11] Hence, while Christians are called to bear witness to God by trying to describe the movement of God, they also must take pains to remind those who listen that what they describe is not the same as its reality. Barth puts the situation succinctly: "As Christians we ought to speak of God. We are human, however, and so cannot speak of God. We ought therefore to recognize both *our obligation and our inability* and by that very recognition give God the glory."[12]

In light of this, Barth concludes there is no element of theological thinking that does not find its ultimate basis in the work and activity of God, which always escapes our comprehension and control. This is not the result of doubt or criticism but rather of the God who is the focal point of our theology. Hence, all assertions and conclusions must be questioned in order to demonstrate their temporary and incomplete nature. The God revealed in Jesus Christ determines that in the work of theology "there are no comprehensive views, no final conclusions and results." There is only the investigation and teaching which is part of the work of theology and which, "strictly speaking, must continually begin again at the beginning in every point. The best and most significant thing that is done in this matter is that again and again we are directed to look back to the centre and foundation of it all."[13] This is a reminder that our best theological work will always fail to do adequate justice to its subject matter and that we must never grow satisfied and complacent with our findings. Instead, in constant dependence on God, we must cultivate the habit of open-ended theology and begin our work again and again at the beginning.

In light of this framework, how should we understand theology so that it is consistent with both the mission of God and the character of God? In spite of all the conversation about the missional

11. Karl Barth, *The Word of God and the Word of Man*, trans. Douglas Horton (London: Hodder and Stoughton, 1928), 282–83.
12. Barth, *Word of God and the Word of Man*, 186.
13. Karl Barth, *Church Dogmatics* 1/2 (Edinburgh: T&T Clark, 1956), 868.

church and missional theology, Benjamin Connor observes that, while use of the term *missional* in conjunction with theology has become ubiquitous, "there really is no shared notion about what missional theology is—to this point there has been no substantive crosscurrent of conversation about the parameters and shape of missional theology."[14] Drawing primarily from the work of Darrell Guder and George Hunsberger, he offers the following provisional definition: "Missional theology is a kind of practical theology that explores in every aspect of the theological curriculum and praxis of the church the implications of the missionary nature of God with the purpose of forming congregations to better articulate the gospel and to live faithfully their vocation to participate in the ongoing redemptive mission of God in their particular context."[15]

What is particularly helpful here is the emphasis on the practical element of missional theology. Because its very purpose is to help congregations participate faithfully in the mission of God, missional theology is inherently focused on life and practice rather than on intellectual articulation and appreciation of the mission of God, though these are certainly important. This focus on the life of a community is a distinctive aspect of missional theology, and thus missional theology must be done in the context of a community committed to participation in the mission of God. While it certainly has an intellectual component, it is never solely an intellectual enterprise.

In keeping with this trajectory I have proposed this definition: Missional theology is an ongoing, second-order, contextual discipline that engages in the task of critical and constructive reflection on the beliefs and practices of the Christian church for the purpose of assisting the community of Christ's followers in their missional vocation to live as the people of God in the particular

---

14. Benjamin T. Connor, *Practicing Witness: A Missional Vision of Christian Practices* (Grand Rapids: Eerdmans, 2011), 11.
15. Connor, *Practicing Witness*, 39.

social-historical context in which they are situated. This definition
has three distinct yet overlapping components:

- *The nature of missional theology*: an ongoing, second-order,
  contextual discipline
- *The task of missional theology*: critical and constructive reflection on the beliefs and practices of the Christian church
- *The purpose of missional theology*: assisting the community
  of Christ's followers in their missional vocation to live as the
  people of God in the particular social-historical context in
  which they are situated[16]

The Nature of Missional Theology

Theology always emerges from a particular set of circumstances
and conditions that give it a particular shape. From the cultural
particularity of Second Temple Galilean Judaism to the passage
of Christian theology and tradition into the thought-forms of
Hellenism and numerous other cultural settings, in every "missionary enterprise and conversion experience, people have met
Christ mediated through cultures—both theirs and the culture of
those who communicated the gospel to them."[17] Lesslie Newbigin
observes that the Bible itself "is a book which is very obviously in
a specific cultural setting. Its language is Hebrew and Greek, not
Chinese or Sanskrit. All the events it records, all the teachings it
embodies, are shaped by specific human cultures."[18]

This reality points to the contextuality of all theological expressions of faith. The sociology of knowledge declares that all
forms of thought are embedded in social conditions, and while

16. This chapter provides a summary of this definition drawn from John R.
Franke, *The Character of Theology: An Introduction to Its Nature, Task, and Purpose* (Grand Rapids: Baker Academic, 2005).
17. González, *Every Tribe and Nation*, 30.
18. Newbigin, *Gospel in a Pluralist Society*, 144–45.

this does not mean that those conditions unilaterally determine them, it does point to their fundamental situatedness. All knowledge is situated. It is influenced and shaped by the social, cultural, and historical settings from which it emerges. As a human endeavor bound up with the task of interpretation, the discipline of theology, like all other intellectual pursuits, bears the marks of the particular contexts in which it is produced. From this perspective, the intent of theology is not simply to set forth, amplify, refine, and defend a timelessly fixed orthodoxy. The questions and contexts that theology seeks to address are constantly shifting. In addition, different people in a given time and place ask different questions.

The African American theologian James Cone puts the matter succinctly: "I respect what happened at Nicea and Chalcedon and the theological input of the Church Fathers on Christology. . . . It is all right to say as did Athanasius that the Son is *homoousia* (one substance with the Father). . . . And I do not want to minimize or detract from the significance of Athanasius' assertion for faith one iota. But the *homoousia* question is not a black question."[19] He goes on to say that Black people do not ask if Jesus is one with the Father; instead they ask if Jesus is walking with them in the midst of their troubles. He reminds us that questions such as those asked and addressed by early Christian writers like Athanasius and others emerged in a different setting, not in the context of the Black experience. He points out that if Athanasius had been an enslaved Black person in America, he would certainly have asked different questions. Without calling into question the value and significance of past theological formulations and affirmations, Cone is simply noting that the setting in which theology is developed has a deep effect on what is produced. His point is that "one's social and historical context decides not only the questions we address to God but also the mode or form of the answers given to the questions."[20]

19. James H. Cone, *God of the Oppressed*, rev. ed. (Maryknoll, NY: Orbis, 1997), 13.
20. Cone, *God of the Oppressed*, 14.

Theology is not a universal language. It is situated language that reflects the goals, aspirations, and beliefs of a particular people, a particular community. No statement of theology can speak for all. Instead, theology is formulated in the context of a particular community of faith and seeks to bear witness to the God to whom faith is directed and the implications of that faith in the context of the specific historical and cultural setting in which it is lived. Because theology draws from contemporary thought-forms in theological reflection, the categories it uses are culturally and historically conditioned.

This is evident from the history of Christian thought in which the expression of theology has taken shape and has been revised in the context of numerous social and historical settings. It has also developed in the process of navigating a number of significant cultural transitions: from a Hebraic setting to the Hellenistic world; from Greco-Roman culture to Franco-Germanic; from the world of medieval feudalism to the Renaissance; from the Renaissance to the Enlightenment; from modernity to postmodernity; and from the colonial context to the postcolonial.

We simply cannot escape from our particular setting and gain access to an objective, transcultural vantage point. All views emerge from some particular location. Hence, all theology is, by its very nature as a human enterprise, influenced by its cultural context. The quest for a transcultural theology is also theologically and biblically unwarranted. Lesslie Newbigin observes that this is the case with the gospel itself: "We must start with the basic fact that there is no such thing as a pure gospel if by that is meant something which is not embodied in a culture." He points out that the meaning of even the simplest verbal statement of the gospel, "Jesus is Lord," is dependent on the content which that culture gives to the word *lord*. How is "lordship" understood in the particular culture in which this idea is proclaimed? The contextual nature of theology brings the relationship between theology and culture into sharp relief. In seeking to address the relationship of theology to its particular circumstances, two approaches that have gained widespread attention are those of correlation and translation.

The *correlationist* tradition follows a model that seeks to explain the content of Christian faith through existential questions that are generally understood as relating to the universal human experience. Because the questions are raised by philosophy through careful examination of human existence, the theologian must first function as a philosopher. Then in a second step, the theologian draws on the symbols of divine revelation to formulate answers to the questions implied in human existence, which philosophy can discover but not answer. The theologian's task is to interpret the answers of revelation so that they remain faithful to the original Christian message while being relevant to the questions asked by contemporary women and men. This certainly provides for substantial engagement with issues pertaining to context, but critics have maintained that it gives too much autonomy and independence to philosophy in relation to theology. Specifically, critics wonder how such an approach, in light of the tensions inherent in finite reason, can be trusted to formulate the right questions. They maintain that the substance and form of the questions set forth by a philosophy, if not revised in the light of Christian thought, will have a distorting effect on the supposedly Christian constructions that emerge from the procedure.

In addition, some have critiqued the correlationist enterprise for its inability to take seriously the emphasis of contemporary cultural anthropology on the specificity and plurality of the human experience. Rather than searching for the characteristics of supposed universal cultural themes, anthropologists are interested in particular cultures. This development in anthropology raises significant challenges to the method of correlation that formulates human universals as the context into which theological constructions are subsequently fitted. Instead, contemporary cultural anthropology invites theologians to focus on the particular and to see theology as a part of a concrete, specific, communally shaped way of life.

Another model for the engagement between theology and culture is the *translation* model. Stephen Bevans identifies this approach as "the most commonly employed and usually the one most people think of when they think of doing theology in context."[21] In this approach, neutral and relative cultural forms become the means by which the absolute, unchanging, supracultural truths of divine revelation and theology are communicated. However, it is important to understand that in the same way as our historical and social context plays a part in the construction of the reality in which we live, so our context influences our understanding of God, our interpretation of the Bible, and the expression of our faith.

The chief difficulty with both of these models is their assumption of some universal meaning structure to communicate theology; they do not acknowledge the particularity of every cultural context and theological formation. Correlationists are prone to prioritize culture through the identification of some universal experience and fit theology into a set of generalized assumptions. In contrast, translationist approaches often overlook the particularity of every understanding of the Christian message and too readily assume a Christian universal that then functions as the basis for the construction of theology, even though it will need to be articulated in the language of a particular culture. This is especially evident in models of translation or contextualization that are based on a distinction between the transcultural gospel and its expression through neutral cultural forms. Yet with few exceptions, most approaches to theology and context that move in the direction of the translation model presuppose the existence of a pure, transcendent gospel.

In spite of their difficulties, these approaches point the way forward. The two models suggest that to be appropriately contextual, theology must employ an interactive process that is both

21. Stephen B. Bevans, *Models of Contextual Theology* (Maryknoll, NY: Orbis, 1992), 37.

correlative and translational while resisting the tendencies of foundationalism.[22] Neither gospel nor culture can function as the primary entity in the conversation and interaction between the two in light of their interpretive and constructed nature; we must recognize that theology emerges through an ongoing conversation involving both gospel and culture. While such an interactive model draws from both methods, it stands apart from both in one crucial way. Unlike correlation or translation, a dynamic and interactional model presupposes neither gospel nor culture as given, preexisting realities that subsequently enter into conversation. Rather, in the interactive process, both gospel and culture are viewed as particularized, dynamic realities that inform and are informed by the conversation itself. Understanding gospel and culture in this way allows us to recognize the dynamic nature of our understanding of the gospel and of the meaning structures through which people in our society make sense of their lives. In such a model, the conversation between gospel and culture should be one of mutual enrichment in which the exchange benefits the church in its ability to address its context as well as the process of theological critique and construction.

Because the situation into which the church bears witness to the message of the gospel is constantly changing, the work of theology is an ongoing process. "The time is past when we can speak of one, right, unchanging theology, a *theologia perennis*. We can only speak about a theology that makes sense at a certain place and in a certain time. We can certainly learn from others (synchronically from other cultures and diachronically from history), but the theology of others can never be our own."[23] No matter how

___

22. *Foundationalism* is a theory concerned with the justification of knowledge. It maintains that beliefs must be justified by their relationship to other beliefs and that the chain of justifications that results from this procedure must not be circular or endless but must have a terminus in foundational beliefs that are immune from criticism and cannot be called into question. For more, see chapter 4 below, under "The Shape of Missional Theology: Beyond Foundations."

23. Bevans, *Models of Contextual Theology*, 4–5.

persuasive, beautiful, or successful past theologies may have been, the church is always faced with the task of bearing witness to the faith in the context of the particular circumstances and challenges in which it is situated. Theology is never completed in a once-for-all fashion: it must continue to wrestle with the challenges of an ever-changing world.

The ongoing and contextual nature of theology suggests that theology is a second-order discipline and highlights its character as an interpretive enterprise. As such, the doctrinal, theological, and confessional formulations of theologians and particular communities are viewed as the products of human reflection on the primary stories, teachings, symbols, and practices of the Christian church and therefore must be distinguished from these first-order commitments of the Christian faith. For example, theological constructions and doctrines are always subservient to the content of Scripture and therefore must be held more lightly. In other words, they are a second-order language in which people try to make sense of the biblical narratives and teachings that are the first-order components of the Christian faith. While this second-order language is helpful and even necessary, it also presents challenges. For instance, it creates conceptual vocabularies and sophisticated forms of argument that often seem far removed from idioms of the Bible.

This second-order language is part of the church's creedal and confessional heritage. Christianity is a confessing religion that has produced a rich tradition of statements of belief. These catechetical and confessional statements arise out of the act of confession, one of the primary and defining activities of the church. In the act of confession, the church seeks, in dependence on the Spirit, to bind itself to the living God and the truth and hope of the gospel of reconciliation and redemption. This act of confession produces affirmations whose purpose is to bear witness to the gospel and promote the ongoing confessional life and activity of the Christian community. Confessional statements and formulas function as servants of the gospel in the life of the church, reflecting convictions concerning the meaning and implications of the primary stories, teachings, symbols, and practices of the Christian church.

When the church attempts to engage in its appointed tasks apart from the act of confession, it runs the risk of losing sight of its relationship to the gospel. This can occur in one of two ways.

First, it can occur through the decision to marginalize the confessional tradition of the church and function as though it did not exist by relegating it to the status of a museum piece. This marginalization of the confessional heritage of the church effectively cuts contemporary communities off from the past action of the Spirit speaking to the churches throughout the ages and detracts from its corporate witness to the gospel.

Second, it can occur through the claim that a particular confessional statement must be viewed as virtually, or even absolutely, infallible. While many Protestants show little regard for the confessional tradition, another segment has continually maintained a very strong, confessional approach to tradition as a vital component of theology. Finding their theological bearings in the authority of the confessions and catechisms of their various traditions, these communities often give evidence of a static, rather than living, view of tradition. As a consequence, the theology that emerges in such circles often belies the contextual nature of all theological formulations.

Each of these approaches is problematic for the missional church. In the first instance, the act of confession is severed from its connection to the past operation of the Spirit. In the second, an awareness of the ongoing need for confession is blunted, while a past confessional formulation is taken, implicitly or explicitly, to be an adequate confession for all times and places. The Christian church's creeds and confessions can best be viewed as an extended series of second-order interpretive reflections on the primary stories, teachings, symbols, and practices of the Christian faith. Like all theological assertions, they are subordinate and provisional.

They are subordinate to God and Scripture. Confessions, creeds, and catechisms are responses to the revelation of God and its witness in Scripture. However, this should not lead to the conclusion that confessions and creeds are merely poor, fallible human attempts to bear witness to the truth of the gospel. Referring to the provisionality of confessions is not an expression of skepticism or an attempt to undermine genuine confession; it simply is a sober consequence of the fact that finite human beings cannot fully comprehend the revelation of God, and an acknowledgment of the need for the ongoing reformation of the church's thought and speech.

The ongoing, second-order, and contextual nature of theology alerts us to the fact that in a real sense, all theology is local—that all attempts at doing theology will be influenced by the particular thought-forms and practices that shape the social context from which it emerges and will bear the distinctive marks of that setting.[24] This means that while theology is genuinely local in the sense that it is shaped and marked by its particular context, it also is responsible in its local iterations to the whole church in its historical and global expressions. The local character of theology must not become the basis for sectarianism in the church. This points us to the task of missional theology.

The Task of Missional Theology

The local nature of theology raises a challenge for the practice of an appropriately catholic theology, the attempt to teach and bear witness to the one faith of the whole church. How do we do theology that is consistent with God's universal mission of love and not simply accommodated to our own aspirations? Lesslie

24. For an extended discussion of the character of local theology, see Robert J. Schreiter, *Constructing Local Theologies* (Maryknoll, NY: Orbis, 1985); and Clemens Sedmak, *Doing Local Theology: A Guide for Artisans of a New Humanity* (Maryknoll, NY: Orbis, 2002).

Newbigin has addressed this question by observing that while a Christian's ultimate commitment is to the gospel and the biblical story, all of us are participants in a particular social setting whose whole way of thinking is shaped by the cultural model of that society in conscious and unconscious ways. We cannot absolutize these cultural contexts without impairing the ability to properly discern the teachings and implications of the gospel. Yet as participants in a particular culture, we are not able to see many of the numerous ways in which we take for granted and absolutize our own assumptions.

Given this situation, Newbigin maintains that the unending task of theology is to be wholly open to the gospel in such a way that the assumptions and aspirations of a culture are viewed in light of the gospel, not the other way around. This leads to expressions of the biblical story that make use of particular cultural models without being controlled by them. This can only be done, he asserts, if Christian theologians are "continuously open to the witness of Christians in other cultures who are seeking to practice the same kind of theology."[25]

In keeping with the ongoing, second-order, and contextual nature of the discipline, the task of theology involves both critical and constructive reflection on the beliefs and practices of the church. Critical reflection involves the careful examination and scrutiny of the church's beliefs and practices to ensure they are coherent with the biblical narratives and commitments of the community and not enslaved to cultural practices and patterns of thinking that are inconsistent with the gospel and the mission of God. It also seeks to ensure that a community's actions do not belie its deepest commitments.

An example of this is found in Paul's letter to the Galatians. In 2:11–14 he recounts the story of challenging Peter about his

---

25. Lesslie Newbigin, "Theological Education in a World Perspective," *Churchman* 93 (1979): 114–15.

actions, which Paul says were inconsistent with the very gospel Peter was proclaiming:

> When Cephas [Peter] came to Antioch, I opposed him to his face, because he stood self-condemned; for until certain people came from James, he used to eat with the Gentiles. But after they came, he drew back and kept himself separate for fear of the circumcision faction. And the other Jews joined him in this hypocrisy, so that even Barnabas was led astray by their hypocrisy. But when I saw that they were not acting consistently with the truth of the gospel, I said to Cephas before them all, "If you, though a Jew, live like a Gentile and not like a Jew, how can you compel the Gentiles to live like Jews?"

In the same way, the church throughout the years has failed to embody practices that are faithful to the message it proclaims. These performative contradictions need to be identified and corrected.

Critical reflection is necessary because of the nature of the church. While the church is guided by the Spirit, it is situated in the midst of human and earthly circumstances, and that reality shapes all that occurs in the church. And in spite of the high calling entrusted to it by God, it often experiences temporal failure in its vocation as the sign, instrument, and foretaste of the kingdom of God. In the midst of this calling to bear faithful witness, the church "passes on its way through history, in strength and in weakness, in faithfulness and in unfaithfulness, in obedience and in disobedience, in understanding and misunderstanding of what is said to it."[26]

Hence, theology engages in an ongoing critical assessment of the beliefs and practices of the church, guided by the Spirit through Scripture, tradition, and culture in order to continually assess its missional faithfulness. This is an aspect of theology to which we must return again and again in a ceaseless effort to ensure that

26. Karl Barth, *Dogmatics in Outline* (New York: Harper & Row, 1959), 10–11.

the proclamation and life of the church are in accordance with the gospel. Faithful critical reflection demands constant attention to the exegesis of Scripture and openness to what one finds in its pages. That said, one of the great challenges to the critical aspect of the theological task is the sheer familiarity, or presumed familiarity, with the biblical text. In addition, patterns of reading and deeply ingrained intuitions and assumptions can make the assertion that we always subject the beliefs and practices of our churches to the teaching of Scripture little more than an abstract and empty formality. In this way, the gospel and the witness of Scripture can become domesticated by the standards of a particular culture or tradition.

Openness to the witness of other Christian communities can provide a context in which our own assumptions and presuppositions can be challenged and corrected where necessary for the sake of the proclamation of the gospel and the mission of the church. From this perspective, and in light of the opportunities and resources available in an increasingly global environment, engagement with the theological reflection and witness of the church in history and in other cultural settings can no longer be viewed simply as a luxury or only as an enterprise for specialists, which most churches can safely disregard and ignore. Rather, it should be viewed as a crucial component of critical theological reflection that seeks to be attentive to the guidance of the Spirit in the church throughout its history and in its contemporary iterations.

The critical aspect of the theological task implies the constructive. The task of theological reflection is not simply to find inconsistencies and make corrections in the beliefs and practices of the community but also to provide insight into appropriate ways of assisting the church to live out its calling in particular settings. Constructive reflection involves the development and articulation of models of Christian faith that are appropriate to the contemporary social-historical context. These models should be faithful to the biblical narratives and teachings, relevant to the contemporary setting, and informed by the traditions of the church. Hence, the sources for such a theology are the canonical Scriptures, the thought-forms of the contemporary social and cultural context, and the traditions of the church.

The goal in this process is to envision all of life in relationship to the triune God revealed in Jesus Christ. That vision emerges through the articulation and practice of biblically normed, culturally relevant, and historically informed models of the Christian faith that express and communicate the biblical story in terms that make sense of it through the use of contemporary conceptual tools. It has become commonplace to use the metaphor of model construction as a way of understanding the theological task.[27] A theological model is a heuristic device by which complex issues and questions can be helpfully delineated and opened up for both expression and critical scrutiny. And while models cannot fully capture all the complexities and nuances of the phenomenon under consideration, they are able to stimulate engagement and interaction with it. They should be viewed "seriously but not literally."[28]

Models are constructions, not exact representations of particular phenomena. For example, the doctrine of the Trinity serves as a model of God and the relationship between the members of the divine fellowship. It does not provide a direct and literal picture of God, but it does, based on God's self-revelation, disclose features of God's character and the divine life. It is a second-order linguistic construction that, while not an exact replica of God,

27. For example, Avery Dulles, *Models of the Church* (Garden City, NY: Doubleday, 1974) and *Models of Revelation* (New York: Doubleday, 1983); John F. O'Grady, *Models of Jesus* (Garden City, NY: Doubleday, 1981); Raymond Collins, *Models of Theological Reflection* (Lanham, MD: University Press of America, 1984); Sallie McFague, *Models of God: Theology for an Ecological, Nuclear Age* (Philadelphia: Fortress, 1987); Elizabeth A. Johnson, *Quest for the Living God: Mapping Frontiers in the Theology of God* (New York: Continuum, 2007); and Bevans, *Models of Contextual Theology.*

28. Ian G. Barbour, *Myths, Models, and Paradigms: A Comparative Study in Science and Religion* (New York: Harper & Row, 1974), 7.

does provide genuine comprehension concerning the nature and character of God. Helpful models function like images and symbols and "provide ways through which one knows reality in all its richness and complexity. Models provide knowledge that is always partial and inadequate but never false or merely subjective."[29]

Models of God and the relationship of God to the created order facilitate engagement and provide accurate insight and understanding without the claim that they provide an exact representation of God. God is transcendent and unique, and categorically different from anything in creation. As the early church theologian Irenaeus once remarked, "God is light and yet unlike any light that we know."[30] As George Hunsinger points out, "God's cognitive availability through divine revelation allows us, Irenaeus believed, to predicate descriptions of God that are as true as we can make them, while God's irreducible ineffability nonetheless renders even our best predications profoundly inadequate."[31] This alerts us to the metaphorical nature of language, particularly with respect to the infinite and transcendent God of the Judeo-Christian tradition. Therefore, we construct models of God that are in keeping with God's self-revelation and that have analogical affinity with the nature and character of God and the relationship between God and the world while recognizing the limitations of all such models.

This leads to a distinction between exclusive and inclusive models. Proponents of exclusive models suggest that the task of theology is to identify the single most appropriate model and employ it to the exclusion of others, even while accepting the analogical character of all models. Inclusive models suggest the importance of multiple perspectives in the exploration and interpretation of theological truth. Stephen Bevans comments that due

29. Bevans, *Models of Contextual Theology*, 30.
30. Irenaeus, *Against Heresies* 2.13.4.
31. George Hunsinger, "Postliberal Theology," in *The Cambridge Companion to Postmodern Theology*, ed. Kevin J. Vanhoozer (Cambridge: Cambridge University Press, 2003), 47.

to "the complexity of the reality one is trying to express in terms of models, such a variety of models might even be imperative" and goes on to suggest that "an exclusive use of one model might distort the very reality one is trying to understand."[32]

In light of the finite character of human knowledge and the infinite divine subject matter of theology, a proper conception of God defies a unique description and requires a diversity of perspectives. All constructions are inadequate on their own and need to be supplemented by other models. This does not preclude the possibility of the adoption of one particular model as the most helpful from a particular vantage point, but as Avery Dulles comments, even this procedure does not require one to "deny the validity of what other theologians may affirm with the help of other models. A good theological system will generally recognize the limitations of its own root metaphors and will therefore be open to criticism from other points of view."[33]

In other words, no one model is able to account for all the diversity of the biblical witness, the diversity of perspectives on it, and the complexity in the interaction between gospel and culture that gives rise to theology. This observation brings us back to the critical aspect of the theological task and leads to the assertion that in the same way that the critical aspect of the theological task gives rise to the constructive, so the constructive gives rise to the critical. The task of theology must involve both critical and constructive reflection in order to bear faithful witness to its unique subject. Hence, the constructive aspect of the theological task involves the articulation of biblically normed, culturally relevant, and historically informed models of the Christian faith that are inherently self-critical and reforming, in keeping with the character of human knowledge and the subject of theology. In addition, the task of theological construction may be characterized

32. Bevans, *Models of Contextual Theology*, 30.
33. Dulles, *Models of Revelation*, 34–35.

as an ongoing conversation we share as participants in the faith community as to the meaning of the symbols through which we express our understanding of the world we inhabit.

The task of missional theology in its various historical, cultural, ethnic, and ecclesial expressions is to offer its particular witness to the whole Christian faith as an ecumenical enterprise for the purpose of contributing to the common task of the whole church to clarify the teaching of the one faith. This means that the voices and perspectives of various traditions and ethnicities are not to be seen as merely serving their own particular communities. Reformed theology is not simply for the Reformed church, nor is Lutheran theology only for Lutherans. Although these theologies arise from particular confessional communities, ultimately they serve the whole church. In the same way, we must not think that Black theology is only for Black people, Asian theology only for Asians, and feminist and womanist theology only for women. These theologies, though they arise from different experiences and are particularly attentive to those experiences, are nevertheless for the whole church. They must inform the thought of all if we are to bear witness to the truth of the gospel and mission of God.

While missional theology always arises out of particular social and historical experiences and contexts, its intent is to serve the whole church precisely by bearing witness from the particularity of those experiences and perspectives to the truth of the gospel on behalf of the whole. Indeed, it is only through this attention to the whole range of human experience in all of its vastness that we are able to perceive the fullness of the gospel and its significance for all of life.

The Purpose of Missional Theology

In addressing the purpose of theology, we are asking the why question. Why do we engage in the task of theology? What is the point and intention of doing theology in the first place? Is it to acquire a proper set of beliefs concerning God? Is it to correct false teaching? Of course, these matters are important, and Scripture identifies each of them as aspects of the Christian life and the work of the church that require attention. However, neither provides an ultimate answer to the question of why we do theology. Why do we need a proper set of beliefs about God, and why might it be important to seek to correct inappropriate teaching? Scripture also provides a number of other assertions that may relate to the purpose of theology. We are called to love God with the entirety of our being, including through the use of our minds (Matt. 22:37); to resist conformity to the patterns of the world and be transformed through the renewing of our minds in accordance with the will of God (Rom. 12:2); to bring every thought into obedience with Christ (2 Cor. 10:5); and to always be prepared to give an answer to any who inquire about the reason for the hope we have in Christ (1 Pet. 3:15). While each of these provides an important perspective on the character of theology, they still do not leave us with an ultimate answer concerning its overarching purpose.

The purpose of missional theology is to cooperate with the Spirit to form witnessing communities that participate in the divine mission by living God's love in the way of Jesus Christ for the sake of the world.[34] The shape of these communities is connected to the missional character of God's eternal life of love reflected in the biblical witness to God's love for the world. This is manifest in the sending of the Son and the Spirit for the purpose of reconciliation and redemption in order that the world might participate in the fellowship of love shared by Father, Son, and Holy Spirit. The church is called to be a provisional demonstration of this fellowship of love in the present that anticipates the fulfillment of God's creative intention in the eschatological consummation of all things.

---

34. On the work of the Spirit speaking in and through the Bible, see Stanley J. Grenz and John R. Franke, *Beyond Foundationalism: Shaping Theology in a Postmodern Context* (Louisville: Westminster John Knox, 2001), 57–92.

Theology participates in this mission by working with the Spirit in the formation and development of a community of persons who believe in the gospel of Jesus Christ and live by it. Missional theology is an outworking of the good news of God's love lived out in the life of a community for the sake of the world. Therefore, the practice of theology from a missional perspective involves "not only greater knowledge of God and God's purposes but more reflective and intelligent participation in those purposes."[35] Of particular importance in the understanding and living out of God's purposes in the world is the call to love one another in response to the love of God: "Beloved, since God loved us so much, we also ought to love one another. No one has ever seen God; if we love one another, God lives in us, and his love is perfected in us" (1 John 4:11–12).

Ephesians 4:12–16 provides a helpful summary of the purpose of theology in keeping with the universal mission of living God's love. Through the Spirit, God gives gifts to the church in order to

> equip the saints for the work of ministry, for building up the body of Christ, until all of us come to the unity of the faith and of the knowledge of the Son of God, to maturity, to the measure of the full stature of Christ. We must no longer be children, tossed to and fro and blown about by every wind of doctrine, by people's trickery, by their craftiness in deceitful scheming. But speaking the truth in love, we must grow up in every way into him who is the head, into Christ, from whom the whole body, joined and knit together by every ligament with which it is equipped, as each part is working properly, promotes the body's growth in building itself up in love.

Missional theology works with the Spirit to equip the Christian community for the works of discipleship, evangelism, and worship

35. Stephen B. Bevans and Roger P. Schroeder, *Constants in Context: A Theology of Mission for Today* (Maryknoll, NY: Orbis, 2004), 1.

in order to build up the body of Christ as it comes to the unity of faith and speaks truth in love. Love is central to this vision: it is in keeping with the centrality of love in the life of God, and it is what God intends for the world.

This love of God lived out in the world is intended to produce peace in accordance with Ephesians 2–3, as discussed in chapter 1 above. The church is called by God to participate in this process as a sign, instrument, and foretaste of the kingdom of God proclaimed by Jesus and as a means of establishing peace on earth. However, the establishment of this peace is paradoxical. It is, on the one hand, a welcome gift from God to be received and cultivated, providing comfort and rest from the often challenging circumstances of life. On the other hand, it is a summons to labor and struggle in solidarity with God and others on behalf of those who are marginalized and oppressed.

We often define "peace" simply as the absence of conflict, but in the biblical tradition it means much more. The Hebrew word for "peace," *shalom*, points not merely to the absence of overt conflict but also to a state of ordered tranquility that is the result of right relationships with God, neighbor, and the whole of creation. It is the interconnectedness of all things for their mutual benefit, something that comes from, and manifests, the goodness of the Creator. Peace is the very intention and gift of God, and it connotes the spiritual and material well-being of individuals and of the community as a whole. It is the result of covenant faithfulness to the ways of God in the world.

The concept of peace in the New Testament builds on the Hebrew notion of *shalom* and intensifies its spiritual dimension as being connected to a life lived in union and solidarity with Jesus, a life that shares his mission of peace and reconciliation through the imitation of his self-sacrificial love for the sake of others. The letter of James contrasts two approaches to life: an earthly, unspiritual, devilish wisdom characterized by envy and selfish ambition, which leads to disorder and wickedness; and wisdom from above that is peaceable, gentle, and willing to yield, which leads to a harvest of righteousness sown in peace. In Scripture, a life lived in accordance with the wisdom that comes from above is described as a life lived in righteousness resulting in an individual state of peace that comes as a gift from God to be enjoyed and continuously cultivated. This is the wonderful peace that is available to everyday disciples of Jesus who live faithful lives in accordance with his teaching. This is the peace that Paul writes about from prison in his letter to the Philippians, the peace that passes all understanding even in the midst of the most difficult circumstances that we encounter in life.

As we saw earlier, the social dimension of *shalom* reminds us that the fullness of peace is never simply an individual matter. *Shalom* describes a vision of a world in which children do not die in infancy, the elderly live productive and dignified lives, and those who build and plant will enjoy the fruit of their labor. This is in stark contrast to the domination societies that were characteristic of the ancient Near Eastern context in which these words were written. Such societies were politically oppressive, economically exploitative, and chronically violent. By common estimates, nearly two-thirds of the production of wealth went to a very small percentage of the population. The gap between the few wealthy elites and the rest of the population had disastrous effects on the majority, condemning them to hardship and struggle and a life expectancy of about half that of the elite class.

The absence of war or overt conflict is no guarantee of peace. The Roman Empire of Jesus's time was also a domination society. While it secured the famous *Pax Romana* (peace of Rome), it also imposed a way of life on its citizens that was the very antithesis of peace: an oppressive political and social structure enforced by violence. In contrast, the Hebrew prophetic tradition proclaimed by Jesus offers a vision of peaceful, harmonious existence in which everyone has enough and no one needs to be afraid.

Jesus's proclamation of this vision points us to the struggle for peace and helps us to understand his words in Matthew 10:34–36: "Do not think that I have come to bring peace to the earth; I have not come to bring peace, but a sword. For I have come to set a man against his father, and a daughter against her mother, and a daughter-in-law against her mother-in-law; and one's foes will be the members of one's own household." How is it that the one spoken of in the Christian tradition as the Prince of Peace can utter these words? Jesus knew that the proclamation of peace for all people would bring him into direct opposition to the principalities and powers of this world in the person of Roman magistrates more interested in preserving the status of their realm than in alleviating its citizens' suffering and oppression. Such challenges to the status quo for the sake of peace, justice, and reconciliation lead to division and conflict by their very nature. The decision to be a disciple of Jesus in our everyday lives brings with it both an unsurpassable peace and a commitment to unremitting struggle on behalf of others that they may live in a just and peaceable world.

Missional theology cooperates with the Spirit in the work of creating a socially constructed world that finds its coherence in Jesus Christ, in accordance with and in anticipation of the "real" world as the Father wills it to be. However, the world as God wills it to be is not a present reality but lies in the eschatological future. Though there is a certain objective actuality to the world, this objectivity is not that of a static actuality existing outside of, and cotemporally with, our socially and linguistically constructed realities. It is not what some might call "the world as it is." Instead, the biblical narratives set forth the objective nature of the world as God wills it. The real world is the future, eschatological world that God will establish in the new creation. Because this future reality is God's determined will for creation, it is far more real, objective, and actual than the present world, which is even now passing away (1 Cor. 7:31). In short, the biblical narratives point to what might be called eschatological realism.

In relating this eschatological realism to the insights of social constructionists, we note that human beings, as bearers of the divine image, are called to participate in God's work of constructing a world in the present that reflects God's own eschatological will for creation. This call has a strongly linguistic dimension due to the role of language in the task of world-construction. Through the constructive power of language, the Christian community anticipates the divine eschatological world that stands at the climax of the biblical narrative in which all creation finds its connectedness in Jesus Christ (Col. 1:17), who is the Word (John 1:1) and the ordering principle of the cosmos. Hence, missional theology may be construed as Christocentric (Christ-centered) in its communitarian focus and Christotelic (Christ-directed) in its eschatological orientation. This eschatological future is anticipated in the present through the work of the Spirit who leads the church into truth (1 John 2:27).

The purpose of theology shaped by the mission of God is to assist the community of Christ's followers in their missional vocation to live out this vision of the people of God in the particular social-historical context in which they are situated. In so doing, the theology aids the church in its calling to be a provisional demonstration of God's will for all people and a foretaste of the kingdom of God.

Doing Missional Theology

Missional theology starts in the life and witness of a community that believes in the gospel and is prepared to live by it. As the community bears witness to the gospel in its particular social location—with all that this implies about the interaction of the community and its setting—missionary encounters and experiences continually shape and challenge the community's conceptions of the gospel and Christian faith and their implications for witness in the world. These encounters and experiences provide the starting point for cultural and theological reflection. This reflection begins with the formulation of questions to be wrestled with and responded to: What is going on in the culture? What needs, desires, concerns, and challenges are reflected in these encounters and experiences? How does the gospel address them? What insight into these situations does Scripture provide? In what ways have Christian communities, past and present, contributed to contemporary situations and challenges? How is God at work in the situation? What is the Spirit saying to the churches?

Because this reflection is the result of lived situations, it will result in missional action as the communities and individuals determine how they will respond to the particular situations and challenges they face. Determination of a course of action will raise additional important questions, prompting further theological reflection: What response constitutes faithfulness to the mission of God? What is the response of love? How might the community need to change? What sacrifices might individuals and the broader community need to make? What impact might particular responses have on the unity of the church? How will dissent be addressed? While this can be construed as a linear process, in fact each part is interactive with the whole (see fig. 3.2 for an illustration of this process).

Figure 3.2
The Process of Missional Theology

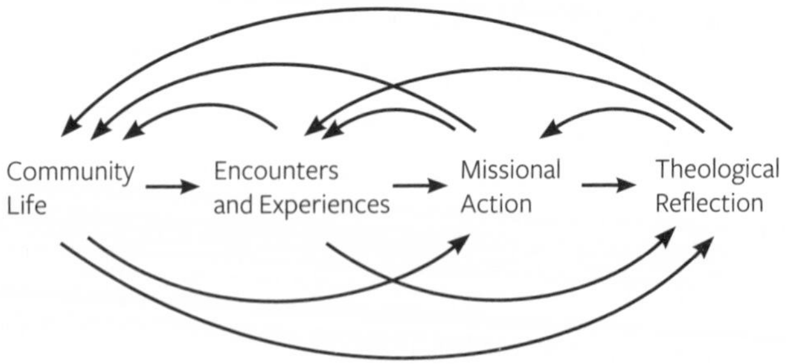

In this process of doing missional theology, we can identify three sources: Scripture, culture, and tradition. Scripture is the principal means by which the Spirit guides the church, and hence the Bible is theology's norming norm. The Bible is, in the words of Newbigin, "that body of literature which—primarily but not only in narrative form—renders accessible to us the character and actions and purposes of God."[36] Through the pages of Scripture, the Spirit communicates the intentions of God for the world, equips the followers of Jesus for participation in those purposes in relation to their social settings, and connects the traditions of past communities with the contemporary proclamation of the gospel. This means that the work of exegesis is critical to the work of theology.

However, as Guder observes, while virtually every Christian tradition affirms the centrality of Scripture for the church, it is possible "to be biblically centered, to expect and to experience biblical preaching, and not to be a church that acknowledges, much less practices, its missional calling."[37] He adds that this is precisely the crisis and the dilemma of much of the Western church: it has appropriated the Scriptures in such a way that central emphasis on the formation for mission has been missed. In this context, it has become possible to hear the gospel as being primarily about what God's grace does for us as individuals. "It is possible to take the Bible seriously, persuaded that it is primarily about one's personal salvation. It is possible to preach the Bible in such a way that the needs of persons are met but the formation of the whole community for its witness in the world is not emphasized. It is, in short, possible to be Bible-centered and not wholeheartedly missional."[38]

In response, missional theology affirms that the texts of Scripture should be read in community from an explicitly missional point of view as a means of forming communities for discipleship and participation in the mission of God. The authors of *Missional*

36. Newbigin, *Foolishness to the Greeks*, 59.
37. Darrell L. Guder, "Biblical Formation and Discipleship," in *Treasure in Clay Jars: Patterns in Missional Faithfulness*, ed. Lois Y. Barrett (Grand Rapids: Eerdmans, 2004), 60.
38. Guder, "Biblical Formation and Discipleship," 60.

Church suggest that to accomplish this, a community should frame
the study of Scripture with missionally incisive questions regarding
the interpretation of biblical texts, particularly those of the New
Testament: "How did this text prepare the early church for its mission, and how does it prepare us for ours? What does this text tell
us about the gospel? What makes it good news? What does this text
tell us about ourselves? About our world? What does this text show
us about the way the gospel is to be made known? How does this
text challenge our organizational forms and functions? How should
our organizational practices change in light of this text? How does
this text challenge us to be converted?"[39] Used in conjunction with
Scripture, questions such as these will work with the Spirit to form
missional communities, but this formation will always be shaped by
the culture in which particular communities are situated.

While Scripture is theology's norming norm, the influence of
culture is all-encompassing, extending to both the production and
the interpretation of the Bible. For some, the inclusion of culture as
a source for theology is inappropriate and out of step with traditional notions of theology. However, as Stephen Bevans observes, in
the history of theology cultural elements are really quite common,
even if not explicitly acknowledged: "While we can say that the
doing of theology by taking culture and social change in culture
into account is a departure from the traditional or classical way of
doing theology, a study of the history of theology will reveal that
every authentic theology has been very much rooted in a particular
context in some implicit or real way."[40] Colin Gunton states the
point succinctly: "We must acknowledge the fact that all theologies
belong in a particular context, and so are, to a degree, limited by
the constraints of that context. To that extent, the context is one of
the authorities to which the theologian must listen."[41] The work of

39. Guder, *Missional Church*, 246.
40. Bevans, *Models of Contextual Theology*, 7.
41. Colin Gunton, "Using and Being Used: Scripture and Systematic Theology,"
Theology Today 47, no. 3 (October 1990): 253.

missional theology calls on us to express the gospel through the language of the culture: the cognitive tools, concepts, images, symbols, and thought-forms through which contemporary people discover meaning, construct their worlds, and form personal identity.

Viewed from this perspective, missional theology includes the attempt to understand and interpret the times in accordance with the purposes of God in order to assist the church to participate more faithfully in the mission of God. The task of listening to the culture involves observation of the various venues and events that give expression to the ethos of our times such as literature, music, film, television, art, newspapers, and magazines, as well as government, courts, universities, and other institutions. In this process, theology not only seeks to respond to the cultural situation but also learns from it. The theological interplay between gospel and culture optimizes our ability to address our context and also can enhance our theological constructions. Indeed, whether directly or, more likely, indirectly, through culture we can gain theological insight. In short, reading our culture can assist us in reading the biblical text so as to hear more clearly the voice of the Spirit in our particular cultural circumstances. In addition to listening for the voice of the Spirit speaking through Scripture, theology must also be attentive to the voice of the Spirit speaking through culture.[42]

This work of the Spirit has produced, and continues to produce, numerous communities that make up the Christian tradition. We often speak glibly of the Christian tradition, but even a cursory glance at the history of the church should make us aware that a multiplicity of Christian traditions make up what we refer to as *the* Christian tradition: Roman Catholic, Orthodox, Lutheran, Reformed, Anglican, Wesleyan, Mennonite, Baptist, and Pentecostal, to name but a few. In addition, considerable diversity marks

42. For a fuller development of this theme, see John R. Franke, "'We Hear the Wonder of God in Our Own Languages': Exploring the Significance of the Spirit's Speaking through Culture," *Cultural Encounters: A Journal for the Theology of Culture* 6, no. 1 (2010): 7–23.

each of these traditions within the larger Christian tradition. Differences among these communities have produced alternative and often competing answers to many important questions concerning Christian faith. Hence, the Christian tradition is best understood as a series of local translations of the gospel and iterations of communal life based on the texts of Scripture in relationship to particular social, historical, and cultural conditions.[43] Taking stock of this multifaceted tradition becomes an important element of the method of missional theology. The Christian tradition is a vast ocean that is beyond full comprehension—the more we are aware of its history and diversity, the more alert we can become to the voice of the Spirit at work in the witness of Christian communities and the "infinite translatability" of the gospel and theology.[44]

This pluriform tradition is accessible in the history of biblical interpretation, theology, worship, and mission; past theological formulations; and the expansion and development of Christianity as a world movement.[45] The diversity and infinite translatability of the Christian tradition is a powerful reminder that it should not be viewed as a weapon to be employed against other communities with which we may be at odds. "A tradition is not a hammer with which to slam dissent and knock dissenters senseless, but a responsibility to read, to interpret, to sift and select responsibly among many competing strands of tradition and interpretations of tradition. If you have a tradition, you have to take *responsibility* for it and its multiplicity."[46] It is to this multiplicity that we now turn our attention.

43. On this theme, see Lamin O. Sanneh, *Translating the Message: The Missionary Impact on Culture* (Maryknoll, NY: Orbis, 2008).

44. Bevans and Schroeder, *Constants in Context*, 2.

45. Of particular importance here is Dale T. Irvin and Scott W. Sunquist, *History of the World Christian Movement*, vol. 1, *Earliest Christianity to 1453*; vol. 2, *Modern Christianity from 1454–1800* (Maryknoll, NY: Orbis, 2001, 2012).

46. John D. Caputo, *Deconstruction in a Nutshell: A Conversation with Jacques Derrida* (New York: Fordham University Press, 1997), 37.

CHAPTER

4

Missional Multiplicity

"But you will receive power when the Holy Spirit has come upon you; and you will be my witnesses in Jerusalem, in all Judea and Samaria, and to the ends of the earth" (Acts 1:8). After speaking these words to his chosen apostles, Jesus was lifted up and taken from their sight. The apostles returned to Jerusalem to wait and pray. On the day of Pentecost, a strong wind came upon them, and they were filled with the Holy Spirit and began to speak in other languages (2:1–4). The text goes on to say that a large and diverse gathering of people who were present for this phenomenon were bewildered because they each heard their own language being spoken. Those who experienced this linguistic phenomenon were reportedly amazed and perplexed and asked one another what it meant (2:5–12).

The meaning of this Pentecostal plurality is significant for understanding the mission of the church to bear witness to the ends of the earth. The action of the Spirit here effectively decenters any particular language or culture with respect to the proclamation of the gospel and the mission of the church. The implication is that no single language or culture is to be viewed as the sole conduit of the gospel message. Christians do not insist that new followers learn the biblical languages; they have made the Bible available to people in different cultures by translating it into their languages. This principle has been a key component in the development of Christian approaches to mission shaped around the notion of plurality and contextuality. Christian historian and missiologist Lamin Sanneh contrasts this approach to mission with that of Islam, which "carries with it certain inalienable cultural assumptions, such as the indispensability of its Arabic heritage in Scripture, law and religion." He asserts that, at its best, Christian witness follows the Pentecostal pattern in the Acts narrative and prefers "to make the recipient culture the true and final locus of the proclamation, so that the religion arrives without the presumption of cultural rejection."[1]

This approach to mission has led to the translation of the Bible into numerous vernacular languages. The complete Bible has been translated into 698 languages, while 1,548 languages have a complete New Testament, and an additional 1,138 have some translated portions of the Bible.[2] The availability of the Bible in these languages has led to the ever-increasing establishment of culturally and socially diverse witnessing communities throughout the world. These new communities are called to live out an alternative way of life in the world as every tribe and nation bears witness to the good news of God's love for all people. In the aftermath of Pentecost, the church emerged as a multifaceted, multidirectional movement in keeping with the calling of the Christian community to bear witness to the ends of the earth. Its development was not, as has often been pictured or implied, from Palestine to Europe to the rest of the world. Rather, it moved from Palestine to Asia,

1. Lamin Sanneh, *Translating the Message: The Missionary Impact on Culture* (Maryknoll, NY: Orbis, 1989), 20.
2. Wycliffe Bible Translators, "Our Impact," accessed February 13, 2020, https://www.wycliffe.org.uk/about/our-impact.

Palestine to Africa, and Palestine to Europe and was immersed in the cultural diversities present in these places. It is a story that must be understood not simply as "the expansion of an institution but as the emergence of a movement, not as simply the propagation of ready-made doctrine but as the constant discovery of the gospel's 'infinite translatability' and missionary intention."[3]

This translatability continually results in fresh adaptations of the Christian faith as the message of the gospel spreads throughout the world across national, tribal, linguistic, and ethnic boundaries, engaging culture after culture, social setting after social setting, and situation after situation. In this missionary engagement of bearing witness, the church continually reinvents itself to meet the challenges of relating the gospel to new peoples and new cultures. The experience and understanding of what it means to be the church arises from this ongoing engagement of the gospel with culture. "There seems to be an inevitable connection, therefore, between the need for Christian mission, on the one hand, and the need for that mission always to be radically contextual. The urgency of mission is linked to the urgency of change, adaptation and translation—in other words, to context."[4] The ongoing engagement of the gospel with cultures of the world results in an irreducible plurality that reflects the missional nature of the Christian community. The very nature of the call to take the good news of the love of God to the ends of the earth and embody it among all peoples and situations for the good of the world leads inevitably to diversity and multiplicity.

Viewed in this light, we see that plurality rather than uniformity characterizes the story of Christianity. The pervasiveness of this missional multiplicity is such that it must be deemed normative in the development of the Christian tradition. This multiplicity is the outworking of the Spirit leading the church into truth in

---

3. Stephen B. Bevans and Roger P. Schroeder, *Constants in Context: A Theology of Mission for Today* (Maryknoll, NY: Orbis, 2004), 3.
4. Bevans and Schroeder, *Constants in Context*, 31.

accordance with the mission and intentions of God. The story of Pentecost is indicative of the Spirit's work and paradigmatic for the spreading of the gospel message.

The upshot of this history is that all churches everywhere, and the theologies they affirm, are "culture churches" and "culture theologies." All bear the marks of their particular cultural settings. All are shaped, in ways both conscious and unconscious, by the assumptions and intuitions that are part of their social and historical contexts, even where they express dissent from aspects of their cultural surroundings. The cultural embeddedness of all articulations of the gospel and all forms of Christian faith and theology leads missiologist Andrew Walls to conclude that no particular group of Christians "has therefore any right to impose in the name of Christ upon another group of Christians a set of assumptions about life determined by another time and place."[5] This poses a challenge to many of the assumptions about mission that have emerged from the Anglo-European Christian tradition. In the words of the authors of *Missional Church*, "The subtle assumption of much Western mission was that the church's missionary mandate lay not only in forming the church of Jesus Christ, but in shaping the Christian communities that it birthed in the image of the church of western European culture."[6]

Thus we have become more aware of the Western church's tendency to construe and articulate the gospel in ways that reflect its particular cultural context. This approach to mission had made the extension and survival of the institutional church its priority. In contrast, understanding the mission of the church as participation in the mission of God more readily makes the church a witness to the gospel and an instrument of the gospel, but not the goal and

5. Andrew F. Walls, *The Missionary Movement in Christian History: Studies in the Transmission of Faith* (Maryknoll, NY: Orbis, 1996), 8.
6. Darrell L. Guder, ed., *Missional Church: A Vision for the Sending of the Church in North America*, The Gospel and Our Culture Series (Grand Rapids: Eerdmans, 1998), 4.

end of the gospel. The extension of God's mission is in calling and sending the church to be a sign, instrument, and foretaste of the kingdom of God in all the cultures and societies in which it participates. This activity is deeply and radically contextual. In the words of Kavin Rowe, the life of the Christian community is the "cultural explication of God's identity."[7]

This cultural explication that arises from the infinite translatability, radical contextuality, and missionary intention of the gospel points as well to the irreducible plurality of the gospel and missional multiplicity. The diversity of the Christian faith is not, as some approaches to church and theology might seem to suggest, a problem that needs to be overcome. Instead, this plurality is part of the divine design and intention for the church as the image of God, body of Christ, and dwelling place of the Spirit in the world. Christian plurality is a good thing, not something that needs to be struggled against, overturned, and corrected.

Plurality, Christian Faith, and the Word of God

Some may see this affirmation of plurality as a capitulation to the mood of contemporary culture. However, it actually emerges from some of the most central claims of Scripture and beliefs that Christians have commonly held over the centuries. Of particular importance is the belief that the Bible is the inspired Word of God and that the teachings and promises it contains are trustworthy (2 Tim. 3:16–17). Connected with this is the belief that God will provide guidance for the church as it goes on its way through the world. God gives wisdom to those who ask (James 1:5). In addition, the Holy Spirit guides the disciples of Jesus into the truth (John 16:13–14).

But if the Bible is the Word of God, given so that all God's people may be thoroughly equipped for every good work, and if

7. C. Kavin Rowe, *World Upside Down: Reading Acts in the Graeco-Roman Age* (New York: Oxford University Press, 2009), 8.

God gives wisdom liberally to those who ask, and if the Holy Spirit is at work guiding the church into all truth, how are we to make sense of the plurality of the church? Why is it that across time and around the world, Christians seeking guidance and understanding concerning the mysteries of life and the hope of the gospel have come away from their Bible studies and prayer meetings with such different conclusions about nearly every aspect of the one faith?

These differences are not merely incidental to the Christian faith: they are at the very core. What is God like? How can we know God? Who is Jesus Christ and how are we to understand his life and mission? What is the gospel? What is the kingdom of God? What is salvation? What is the Bible and how are we to interpret and understand it? What is the church? What is the ultimate destiny of human beings? The list goes on and on. The fact is that on matters as central to the faith as these, not all Christians agree on the answers.

Several possible answers are readily available to account for the existential reality of Christian plurality. Perhaps the Bible is not really inspired by God. Maybe it is simply a collection of documents that contains mutually exclusive perspectives that render the biblical canon insufficient for the purpose of guiding and equipping the Christian community for common witness in the world. Certainly many individuals have argued along these lines. Perhaps God is less generous in dispensing wisdom than is suggested in Scripture, or maybe the promise that the Spirit would guide the church into truth is idealistic wishful thinking. Another possibility is that a certain segment of the church has grasped the truth and the rest of the church needs to repent of its errors and follow along. It would not be difficult to find adherents among the numerous communities of Christian faith who would be well prepared and quite pleased to make such an argument on behalf of their particular tradition. From the perspective of the historic Christian tradition, though, none of these answers is sufficient. Christians have confessed that Scripture is inspired and given to the church as a means of grace in guiding belief and practice; that God does not skimp on the promise to provide wisdom; and that the Holy Spirit is in fact guiding the whole church, in all of its diverse manifestations, into the fullness of truth that is the living God revealed in Jesus Christ.

Of course, these convictions about Scripture, God, and the Holy Spirit are matters of faith not subject to demonstrable proof. Yet they form some of the central working assumptions that have shaped classical Christian thinking and are well established in Scripture and among Christian communities, past and present. In other words, in seeking to account for the multiplicity of the church, we should do so with an outlook that presumes these core convictions to be true rather than jettison confidence in Scripture, the generosity of God in the provision of wisdom, or the promised guidance of the Spirit.

The claim that the church and theology are properly characterized by plurality and multiplicity should not be taken to mean that everything that goes on in the church is therefore appropriate as a manifestation of diversity. We must bear witness to the faith, commend sound doctrine, and oppose false teaching. Some claims and assertions about Christian belief and practice are wrong and need to be resisted and refuted. False teaching must be identified and challenged. The Bible is clear about this. Leaders are called to "have a firm grasp of the word that is trustworthy in accordance with the teaching, so that [they] may be able both to preach with sound doctrine and to refute those who contradict it" (Titus 1:9). On the other hand, not all disputes are profitable for the church: "But avoid stupid controversies, genealogies, dissensions, and quarrels about the law, for they are unprofitable and worthless. After a first and second admonition, have nothing more to do with anyone who causes divisions, since you know that such a person is perverted and sinful, being self-condemned" (3:9–11).

The claim is not that anything goes but rather that faithful Christian witness in keeping with the mission of God will be characterized by irreducible plurality and will result in missional multiplicity. This missional multiplicity arises from the act of doing theology in keeping with the mission of God. If diverse Christian communities are missionally faithful to the places and contexts in which they are situated, their beliefs and practices will constitute a manifold witness to the gospel. This is entirely consistent with Christian commitments concerning revelation, Scripture, and Christian tradition. Each of these elements is part of the expression of the Word of God in the world.

The Word of God is always an act God performs or an event in which God has spoken, speaks, and will speak. As human beings, we encounter and engage this divine act or event through the Spirit-inspired and Spirit-guided human means of Scripture and its proclamation and practice in the life of the church. From this perspective, we encounter the Word of God in three forms: the act of revelation itself, the Spirit-inspired attestation and witness to revelation in the words of the prophets and the apostles contained in Scripture, and the Spirit-guided proclamation of that witness in the life of the Christian community.

It is important to remember that here we are speaking of three different forms of the one Word of God and not three different Words of God. It may help to imagine three concentric circles that represent three movements in the communication and reception of the Word of God. The innermost circle is the Word of God as divine speech-act authored and spoken by God. However, this divine speech is represented to us and made expressible and approachable through the human and creaturely speech-acts contained in Scripture (the second circle) and the proclamation of the church (the outermost circle). These human speech-acts are appointed by God to be the bearers and witnesses of God's self-revelation in Jesus Christ by the power of the Spirit. Hence, the Word of God may be described as the Word revealed (the circle at the center), the Word written (the second circle), and the Word proclaimed (the outer circle). (See fig. 4.1.) Insofar as the Word of God may be equated with truth, we may also speak of these as truth revealed, truth written, and truth proclaimed.

Figure 4.1
The Word of God in Three Forms

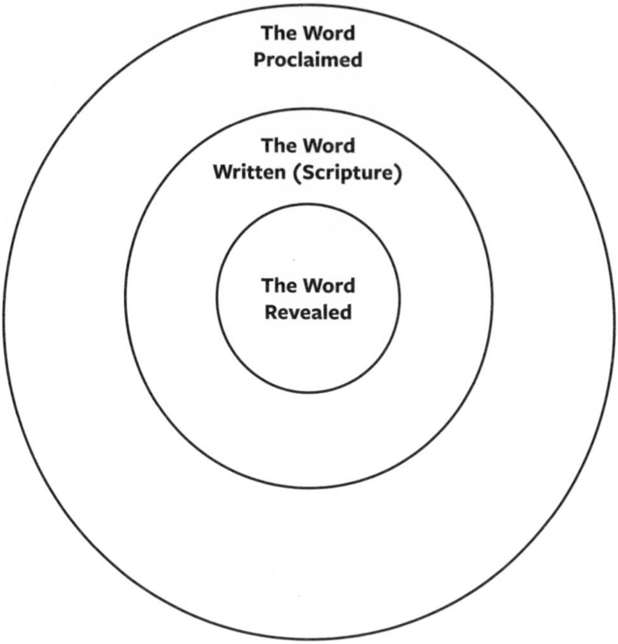

**The Word
Proclaimed**

**The Word
Written (Scripture)**

**The Word
Revealed**

Revelation

In our discussion of the Trinity, we asserted earlier that the life of God is characterized by both plurality-in-unity and unity-in-plurality. In other words, difference is part of the life of God who is love and lives in the active relations of giving, receiving, and sharing love. The Father is not the Son or the Spirit; the Son is not the Father or the Spirit; and the Spirit is not the Father or the Son. This means that in the life of God is the experience of that which is different, other, not the same.

There is an implicit question bound up in the confession that God is triune and lives from all eternity in a social, communal fellowship characterized by love, unity, plurality, and mission: On what basis is this conviction to be affirmed? The Christian answer to this question is revelation. As we conduct our lives, the One who is love and truth speaks to us as our creator and sustainer in order to provide guidance and direction with respect to both belief and practice. This aspect of Christian teaching affirms that God communicated truth to human beings through the free and gracious act of self-revelation in Jesus Christ, as attested in Scripture. The purposes of revelation are to draw creatures into relationship with their creator, invite them to share in the love and fellowship of God, and invite them to participate in the divine mission of love and reconciliation.

In addressing the notion of revelation, it is important to remember one of the central ideas of the Christian tradition: God is God and we are not. The Bible lays out a number of distinctions between creator and creature. In Isaiah 55:8 we are told that God's thoughts are not our thoughts and that our ways are not God's. Second Peter 3:8 declares that for God a day is like a thousand years, and a thousand years are like a day. The Christian tradition has concluded from these and many other texts that the infinite God is radically different from finite creatures. This infinite qualitative distinction means that even revelation is not able to provide human beings with a knowledge that exactly corresponds to that of God. It also points to the accommodated character of all human knowledge of God.

In articulating an understanding of revelation, it is vital to keep the infinite qualitative distinction between God and ourselves at the forefront of our concerns, lest we fall into the idolatry of imagining that our thoughts and conceptions of God and truth correspond to those of God. As finite creatures, we are not able to grasp ultimate reality and truth as God knows those to be. This gives rise to the theological adage *finitum non capax infiniti*—the finite cannot comprehend the infinite.

In order to respect this reality while still affirming that God has been made known in the act of revelation, John Calvin, one of the most influential theologians in Christian history, appeals to the notion of divine accommodation: in the process of revelation, God "adjusts" and "descends" to the limited capacities of human beings and "lisps" to us, as adults do to infants, in order to be made known. Apart from such accommodating action, the knowledge of God would, by its very nature, be beyond the capabilities of human creatures to grasp due to the limitations that arise from our finite character.[8] These limitations of our cognitive and imaginative faculties extend also to the very modes by which revelation is communicated to and received by us. The human reception of revelation is a necessary component of the act of revelation and therefore an integral aspect of our talk about the Word of God and our understanding of truth. Revelation is completed when humans hear the Word of God and receive it in faith and obedience. This human dimension is not contributed independent of the event of the Word, nor can the event of the Word be considered in abstraction from the communal and cultural plurality that characterizes its human reception.

This has significant implications for our understanding of the accommodated character of revelation. For instance, language is contingent on the contexts and situations that give rise to particular vocabularies that shape and are shaped by the social circumstances in which they arise. Each language is a particular conceptual scheme that lacks the capacity and universality required to provide a description of God or ultimate truth that can be thought of as absolute. The plurality and flexibility of particular vocabularies are pointed reminders of the perspectival nature of language itself.

In making this assertion, we can appeal to the ecumenical Christian tradition and the conclusions of the Council of Chalcedon in

8. John Calvin, *Institutes of the Christian Religion* 1.13.1.

451. The Chalcedonian Definition affirms that the divine nature
of Jesus remains divine even in the context of its relationship with
human nature, and Jesus's human nature remains human even in
the context of its relationship with the divine nature. One of the
implications of this formulation is the denial of the divinization
of the human nature of Jesus. Since the human nature employed
as the medium of revelation is not divinized, it remains subject
to its historically and culturally conditioned character. By analogy, we can posit that what is true of the human nature of Jesus
Christ with respect to divinization is also true of the words of
the prophets and apostles in Scripture. The use that God makes
of the creaturely medium of human speech and language in the
inspiration and witness of Scripture does not entail its divinization. Language, like the human nature of Jesus, remains subject
to historical, social, and cultural limitations and contingencies
inherent in its creaturely character, and they do not compromise
its suitability as a medium for the Word of God.

This means that while God's use of language in the act of self-
revelation allows us to speak in authentically informative ways
about God, we still must acknowledge the inherent mystery
and otherness of God even in the act of bearing witness to God
though our speech. The early church theologian Irenaeus captured this idea by asserting that while it is true and faithful to say
that God is light, it is also true that God is unlike any light that
we know.[9] "God's cognitive availability through divine revelation
allows us, Irenaeus believed, to predicate descriptions of God that
are as true as we can make them, while God's irreducible ineffability nonetheless renders even our best predications profoundly
inadequate."[10] Hence, our affirmation of God as light provides
us with a measure of genuine understanding about God but does

9. Irenaeus, *Against Heresies* 2.13.4
10. George Hunsinger, "Postliberal Theology," in *The Cambridge Companion to
Postmodern Theology*, ed. Kevin J. Vanhoozer (Cambridge: Cambridge University
Press, 2003), 47.

not eradicate the infinite qualitative distinction between us and God.

In other words, in the act of revelation God does not break through and negate the situatedness that is part of the human condition. Instead, God has chosen to enter into and participate in the limitations of that condition in the act of revelation as a means of accommodation to the finitude of human creatures. In keeping with the conviction that God speaks, we can affirm the reality of ultimate or transcendent truth even as we acknowledge the interpretive character of human knowledge. At the same time, even if we cannot know reality exhaustively or perfectly, we are able to know something about it by virtue of the grace of divine revelation. This understanding helps us to account for the rich variety of metaphors found in Scripture to describe the living God.

In this conception of human language as a vehicle of analogical reference for God, we must distinguish between the act of divine self-revelation and the finite human witness to that revelation. Both are part of the event of the Word of God, but the human witness to revelation always remains subject to the limitations of its creaturely character. This is true even of the divinely inspired texts of Scripture. We might express the distinction in the following way: the truth as God experiences it and knows it to be is capital T (or ultimate) Truth; the inspired witnesses to truth enabled by divine revelation contained in the human speech-acts of Scripture are situated and fragmentary and are therefore small t truth. By inspiration they bear a proper relationship to God, but inspiration does not enable them to transcend their limitations as a finite creaturely medium. Hence, in this analogy they always are and will remain small t truth, because only God has the knowledge of ultimate Truth.

In this framing, we acknowledge that all human knowledge, experience, and communication are situated in particular circumstances, and these circumstances have a significant effect on the character and content of human experience and knowledge. Only the living God transcends the limitations of time and place that are characteristic of finitude.[11] It is from this perspective that we turn our attention to Scripture.

Scripture

The notion of divine accommodation means that in fulfilling its purpose to form witnessing communities, Scripture functions like a map that effectively guides our journey into the mission of God. It need not be photographically precise or drawn exactly to scale. It is enough that it pragmatically points us in the right direction. The application of divine accommodation to Scripture as the written Word of God points to the contextual character of the Bible and suggests an important element in the way in which Scripture is truth. Scripture functions as the Spirit-inspired attestation and witness to the self-revelation of God through the creaturely medium of the words of the prophets and apostles. These words are embedded in a socially constructed linguistic context.

One of the entailments of the contextual character of the Bible as an inspired witness to the event of revelation is its plurality. Canonical Scripture is itself a diverse collection of witnesses or, put another way, a manifold witness to the revelation of divine truth. In fact, the Bible is not so much a single book as it is a collection of authorized texts written from different settings and perspectives. Each of the voices represented in the canonical collection maintains a distinct point of view that emerges from a particular time and place. In other words, the Bible is polyphonic, made up of many voices.

The self-revelatory speech-act of God is received among diverse communities over long periods of time and in a plurality of cultural settings. The human reception and response is shaped by

11. For a more detailed discussion, see Merold Westphal, *Overcoming Ontotheology: Toward a Postmodern Christian Faith* (New York: Fordham University Press, 2001), 75–88.

the communal and cultural settings in which revelation occurs. The plurality of revelation is received in a plurality of cultural settings, and from these diverse contexts it is expressed and proclaimed to others over the course of history in accordance with the sending of the church into the world as a representative of the sign, instrument, and foretaste of the kingdom of God. Scripture paradigmatically reflects this plurality and diversity. It is the constitutive and normative witness for the formation and proclamation of Christian community. At the same time, it is also the first in an ever-expanding series of presentations of the Christian faith throughout history. In this multifaceted and diverse collection of writings, each offers a distinct perspective that contributes to the whole such that none of the works included can be understood properly apart from their relation to the others. The Bible contains a variety of literary forms such as narrative, law, prophecy, wisdom, parable, epistle, and others. And within each of these forms we find the expression of numerous canonical perspectives.

In addition to diverse literary forms, Scripture contains diverse law codes, chronologies, ethical and theological assertions, and four Gospel accounts. The presence of four different Gospel accounts offers the most straightforward and significant demonstration of plurality in the biblical canon. Matthew, Mark, Luke, and John each express a distinctive perspective on the life and ministry of Jesus, and their inclusion alerts us to the pluriform character of the gospel. This stands as a powerful reminder that the witness of the Christian community to the gospel of Jesus Christ can never be contained in a single universal account. Instead it is always perspectival, always characterized by a diversity of forms, in keeping with the tradition of the biblical canon. In light of that tradition, the early church resisted attempts to harmonize the Gospels into one single account. The fourfold witness of the Gospels of Matthew, Mark, Luke, and John indicates the irreducibility of the gospel of Jesus Christ to a single account. Attempts to systematize the gospel, to reduce it to a manageable and

formulaic form, are doomed to failure in the face of the canonical
witness. A true harmony of the Gospels is neither attainable nor
desirable.

Like the problematic notion of a cultural melting pot in which
numerous distinct cultures come together and form one new universal culture made up of all the others, something of value is
always excluded. When we attempt to ease the difficulties of the
multiple perspectives in Scripture to make matters more compact,
clear, and manageable, we suffer the loss of plurality and diversity
that is woven into the very fabric of Scripture and, by extension,
the divine design of God. This reminds us that a single description of the Christian faith can never be sufficient for all. The
multiplicity and plurality of the biblical witness stands against
such a notion.

True "catholic" or "universal" faith is pluralistic. "It is 'according to the whole,' not in the sense that it encompasses the
whole in a single, systematic, entirely coherent unit, but rather
in the sense that it allows for the openness, for the testimony
of plural perspectives and experiences, which is implied in the
fourfold canonical witness to the gospel."[12] The multiplicity of
the canonical witness to the gospel is not incidental to the shape
of the community from which it emerged under the guidance of
the Holy Spirit and which it envisions for the future. Attempts to
suppress the plurality of the canonical witness by means of an
overarching, universalistic account lead to serious distortions of
the gospel and the community that is called to bear witness to it.
The plurality of forms and perspectives embedded in the biblical
witness suggests that no single voice or interpretive approach will
be able to do justice to this diversity.

In relating these diverse forms as the Word of God, it is important to envision their plurality-in-unity and unity-in-plurality.

12. Justo L. González, *Out of Every Tribe and Nation: Christian Theology at the
Ethnic Roundtable* (Nashville: Abingdon, 1992), 22.

Again, this plurality should not be construed as leading to an "anything goes" sort of relativism. As stated at the outset, the Christian conviction that God speaks rules out this sort of approach, and the acknowledgment of diversity and plurality in the Bible must not be used as an attempt to support such a perspective. In addition, as witness to the revelatory speech-act of the triune God, the plurality of Scripture should not be used as a denial of the unity of the canon. In keeping with the conviction that the Bible is inspired by the Spirit for the purpose of bearing witness to the self-revelation of God and guiding the church into truth, Christians affirm that the Bible constitutes a unity as well as plurality. But this unity is a differentiated unity expressed in plurality.

As such, the Bible has given rise to a variety of meanings and interpretations that are derived from exegesis, theology, and the particular social and historical situations that have shaped its interpreters. As we seek to read the Bible as a unity-in-plurality and plurality-in-unity, we should expect a variety of models and interpretations due to the very nature of the canonical texts themselves. Scripture itself authorizes multiple perspectives within a set of possibilities that are also appropriately circumscribed by the shape and content of the canon. The point here is not that anything goes but rather that within the framework of the biblical canon we should expect plurality.

As the Word of God and normative witness to revelation, Scripture consists of inspired human speech-acts that bear authentic witness to the divine speech-act of the event of revelation, which is itself characterized by plurality. Scripture is truth written, and its pages bear manifold witness to the plurality of truth. As the Word of God and paradigmatic human and creaturely witness to the event of revelation, Scripture also invites greater plurality than that contained in its pages in order that, under the guidance of the Holy Spirit, the witness of the church to the gospel may be continually expanded to all the nations in keeping with the mission of God.

Tradition

This missional multiplicity has resulted in numerous expressions of Christian faith around the world and is the outworking of the expansion and proliferation of the Word of God. The connection of the Christian tradition with the Word of God is a significant element in comprehending the work of the Spirit leading the church into truth and the multiplicity that is an inherent part of that work. Tradition begins with some contingent historical starting point, most often a text or a set of related texts, and develops from this starting point as a historically extended, socially embodied argument as to how best to interpret and apply the formative texts. We can conceive of the Christian tradition as the history of the interpretation and application of Scripture by the Christian community as it listens to the voice of the Spirit speaking through the text. The Christian tradition is composed of the church's historical attempts to explicate and translate faithfully the first-order language, symbols, and practices of the Christian faith, arising from the interaction among community, text, and culture, into the various social and cultural contexts in which that community has been situated.

In this understanding, tradition is viewed not as static but rather as a living, dynamic concept in which development and growth occur. The tradition is thus characterized by both continuity and change as the faith community, under the guidance of the Spirit, grapples with the interaction between Scripture and the particular challenges of changing contexts and situations. To sum up the organic process described in the previous chapter, missional action results from the encounters and experiences that arise in the relationship between the church and the wider community in which it is situated; those encounters and experiences are formed into confessional and practical explications of the gospel. Ultimately, this establishes and expands the traditions of the church.

Insofar as the tradition of the Christian church is the product of the Christian community's ongoing reflection on the biblical message, it is in many respects an extension of the authority of Scripture. The witnesses to God's redemptive activity coupled with the basic teachings and practices of the early Christian community constitute the faith delivered once for all to the saints (Jude 3). This sense of passing on the teachings of the community from generation to generation is the most basic expression of the operation of tradition. Although this commitment to pass on "the faith once delivered to the saints" is an important component of the Christian tradition, it can also be misconstrued and as a consequence used as the basis for oversimplifying a complex phenomenon.

The assumption that tradition comprises an unchanged body of Christian doctrines articulated by the ancient church for all time fails to comprehend properly the dynamic character of tradition. By its very nature, tradition is dynamic within the life of the faith community. The Christian community has always been concerned with the task of proclaiming the message of the gospel to the whole world in order that all people might know and experience the love of God. In keeping with this concern, the church has established communities of believers throughout the world. Consequently, the Christian church has been located in a variety of social, historical, and cultural contexts, and it has faced numerous challenges because of that. These challenges have required the church to exercise wisdom and creative judgment in addressing questions in a manner that best promotes its mission to proclaim the gospel and establish communities of Christ's disciples.

A canonical example of this activity is the story of the Jerusalem Council in Acts 15. Here the Christian community in Jerusalem addresses the cultural issues raised by the conversion of gentiles and their coexistence in the community of the new covenant with ethnic Jews who were concerned to preserve their social distinctiveness. The conclusion of the gathering is that circumcision, a central practice of covenant keeping with the God of Abraham, would not be required of gentile converts. The Jerusalem Christians conclude that the gentiles, in order to be faithful participants in the covenant that God made with Abraham, need not be circumcised, an apparent requirement of Scripture. This is an example of the contextual innovation that arises in the outworking of Christian tradition in missional perspective. It is composed of an ongoing deposit of guidance and wisdom emerging from the dynamic movement of the community under the Spirit's guidance.

The multicultural character of the Christian community alerts us to an additional insight about tradition. As we have observed, all expressions of the faith are contextualized. This includes not only the confessions, creeds, and theological constructions of the church but also the content of the biblical documents themselves. All texts of the Christian faith were formulated within the social, cultural, linguistic, and philosophical frameworks of the times in which they were produced. This observation alerts us to the incarnational character of the Bible and the challenges of contextualizing its message into new, varied, and changing settings and calls for a multifaceted understanding of the tradition of the church as a source for theology.

The Christian tradition, viewed as a series of local theologies, serves as a resource for theology, not as a final arbiter of theological issues or concerns. It provides hermeneutical context or trajectory for the theological task. The history of Christian theology, past theological formulations, the history of Christian worship, and the practices of the Christian community all serve to assist the church in the task of proclaiming the faith in contemporary settings.

In light of the diverse and pluriform history of the church, we must conclude that the basic shape of this hermeneutical trajectory is multiplicity. For an illustration, we can appeal to the differences between Roman Catholicism, Eastern Orthodoxy, and

Protestantism and the pluralities in each of these ecclesial traditions. But this only scratches the surface of the differences among various Christian communities throughout history and in the present day. Even a cursory glance at the *Handbook of Denominations in the United States* will underscore this point.[13] Further, this does not account for the vast plurality of global Christianity. Over 20,000 distinct Christian communities or movements do not identify as Roman Catholic, Eastern Orthodox, or Protestant.[14] This vast pluriform multiplicity constitutes the Spirit-intended shape of faithful Christian expression. This challenges the notion that the great tradition of the church can be identified as those things believed everywhere, always, and by all.

Through the ages, Christians from a wide variety of social and cultural locations have offered various affirmations and denials to confess their faith in the God revealed in Christ and declare their commitment to participate in the divine mission. In so doing they join all who have confessed the Christian faith throughout history. Because Christians are participants through Jesus Christ and the Spirit of God in this continuous historical community, the history of its theological and confessional traditions should be an ongoing conversation partner as we offer our own confession. In this way we seek to maintain a certain theological and confessional unity with the church of the past even in the midst of our diversity.

At the same time, however, we must remember that historical confessions of faith were articulated in particular times and places. If Christians are not simply to parrot past confessions in new and changing circumstances, then new ways of confessing the Christian faith are needed; no confession can serve a once-for-all

13. Roger E. Olson, Frank S. Mead, Samuel S. Hill, and Craig D. Atwood, eds., *Handbook of Denominations in the United States*, 14th ed. (Nashville: Abingdon, 2018).

14. David B. Barrett, George T. Kurian, and Todd M. Johnson, eds., *World Christian Encyclopedia: A Comparative Survey of Churches and Religions in the Modern World*, 2 vols., 2nd ed. (New York: Oxford University Press, 2001), 1:16–18.

function. This is especially so in light of the Spirit's ongoing work in the life of the church. The Spirit is guiding the community of faith into the truth, purposes, and intentions of God. These purposes and intentions are a divine goal anticipated in the present through the life and witness of the church but will be fully realized only at the eschatological consummation of all things. Hence, the tradition of the church, made up of the numerous communities that form it and that constitute its plurality in keeping with its missional vocation, must always be understood as contextual, interpretive, and provisional in character.

In the Spirit's work, Scripture is the norm for Christian faith and life, while the tradition of the Christian community, expressed in beliefs and practices, provides a crucial context and trajectory for proclamation. This proclamation responds to the current situation while also remaining in continuity with the life and witness of the church in its historical and global manifestations. This pluralistic tradition is an important element of the ongoing proclamation of the church in which the past events of the guidance of the Spirit are taken into account for the work of the present.

Theological reflection must be renewed constantly as part of the church's ongoing witness to the revelation of God in Christ. However, in this ongoing work of renewal, attention must be given to the theological tradition of the church as the witness of past attempts to hear God speaking in Scripture. For Karl Barth, the notion of theology as theology for the church means that the

> theology of past periods, classical and less classical, also plays a part and demands a hearing. It demands a hearing as surely as it occupies a place with us in the context of the Church. The Church does not stand in a vacuum. Beginning from the beginning, however necessary, cannot be a matter of beginning off one's own bat. We have to remember the communion of the saints, bearing and being borne by each other, asking and being asked, having to take mutual responsibility for and among the sinners gathered together

in Christ. As regards theology, also, we cannot be in the Church without taking as much responsibility for the theology of the past as for the theology of our present.[15]

The task of taking responsibility for the theology of the past means taking responsibility for the plurality of the Christian tradition and embracing it. It also involves raising questions concerning the ways in which it has failed through hegemonic and institutional structures that have hindered the formation of the diversity that is appropriate to the life of the global and historical community.

The church's ongoing corporate confession and proclamation constitute its diverse and manifold witness to the truth of the gospel of Jesus Christ in its various social and historical embodiments. Lamin Sanneh concludes: "It follows from this theological insight that Christianity is not intrinsically a religion of cultural uniformity, and that in its historical expansion it has demonstrated that empirically by reflecting the tremendous diversity and dynamism of the peoples of the world. Christian pluralism is not just a matter of regrettable doctrinal splits and ecclesiastical fragmentation, but rather of variety and diversity within each church tradition."[16]

The ongoing engagement of the gospel with the cultures of the world means, as affirmed in the previous chapter, that the work of theology is never completed. It results in an ongoing and irreducible plurality that reflects the missional nature of the Christian community to take the good news of the love of God proclaimed in the gospel of Jesus Christ to the ends of the earth and embody it among all peoples and situations for the good of the world. This has produced, and will continue to produce, the

15. Karl Barth, *Protestant Theology in the Nineteenth Century*, new ed. (Grand Rapids: Eerdmans, 2002), 3.

16. Lamin Sanneh, *Whose Religion Is Christianity? The Gospel beyond the West* (Grand Rapids: Eerdmans, 2003), 130.

missional multiplicity that is the very nature and essence of the historic Christian faith.

The missional multiplicity that emerges, with respect to truth, from the three forms of the Word of God—revelation, Scripture, and tradition—is illustrated in figure 4.2. The Truth at the center represents truth as God knows it to be—ultimate truth characterized by trinitarian diversity-in-unity and unity-in-diversity. This Truth is made known in the world through the divine act of revelation accommodated to human finitude. The first band of small *t*'s represents the inspired witness to divine revelation contained in the texts of Scripture. These are situated and fragmentary without ceasing to be true and faithful witnesses to revelation. The second band of *t*'s represents the ever-expanding witness of the church (based on the revelation of God and the witness of Scripture), sent into the world by Jesus and entrusted with the ministry of the gospel. This work of witness and proclamation, preserved in the tradition of the church, is also a form of the Word of God.

Figure 4.2
Multiplicity and truth

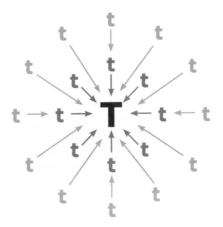

The inner band of *t*'s represents Scripture, and the outer band the church's witness.

Four concluding points. First, the arrows coming from each band of *t*'s indicate the shared vocation of both Scripture and the church to bear faithful witness to the ultimate Truth made known in revelation. Second, the band of *t*'s representing Scripture is closer to the center to indicate its primacy over the witness of the church. As the first in a series of ever-expanding witnesses to the truth, Scripture maintains a unique authority in relation to the tradition of the church (without denying that the tradition of the church is itself an authoritative source for theology). Third, the outer band of *t*'s is always expanding as the church continues to be faithful to its task of bearing witness to the truth of the gospel in every place and situation. Fourth, the plurality of truth illustrated here does not mean that there is also not falsehood or error in the witness of the church. It simply means that in the economy of God the church has been entrusted with bearing witness to the truth of the gospel and it has, through the power of the Spirit, often been faithful to that task even as it has also been guilty of many failures and shortcomings. These failures do not undermine the plurality and multiplicity intended by God in the missional witness of the church.

The Shape of Missional Theology: Dialogical

In imagining the shape of missional theology, we can learn from dialogical approaches to faith that are intentional about including diverse perspectives, particularly those that are underrepresented. This practice bears faithful witness to the event of the Word of God; the plurality of revelation, Scripture, and tradition; the provisional nature of all theological conclusions; and the concern for justice and equality. An example of this intentional approach is found in *Out of Every Tribe and Nation: Christian Theology at the Ethnic Roundtable*, in which Justo González describes the conversations among ethnic minority theologians who gathered to examine various topics of traditional theology from their own perspectives and "enter into dialogue with each other and with traditional theology, seeking a better and deeper understanding of the gospel of Jesus Christ."[17]

González describes the gathering as a celebration of discovery in which the participants shared lively and exciting theological discussions that produced the experience of theological discovery in the midst of their diversity. In addition, they experienced the pleasure of discovering each other as they shared and came to understand one another's hopes and pains as well as the faith that animated their lives. The summary of the conversations from the gathering that make up the published volume is intended as an invitation to readers to both celebrate and share in the participants' discovery. It is a discovery that is vital for the witness of the gospel in the midst of a culture divided by racism, classism, and sexism. Tragically, these forces have also shaped the church. Missional theology is intentional about addressing these divisions and overturning them in keeping with the establishment of a community where everyone has enough and no one needs to be afraid.

Yet, as González observes, the task is not easy, because in the world and in the church there are "powerful forces arrayed against such a discovery. There are the forces of inertia, parochialism, and racism, which push people in our society to stay among others 'of their own kind.' And there are the forces of self-interest, for a true discovery would force us to deal more justly with one another." Nevertheless, this is the task to which the God of mission has called the church in order to represent the image of God in the world as a witness to the character of God and the gospel of Jesus Christ. The difficulty of this calling is that it "goes against the grain of our imbedded cultural racism, against many of our own self-interests, and against much of the current political trend. But God has never called the church to easy tasks. . . . It is the

17. González, *Every Tribe and Nation*, 15.

tasks that the world deems impossible that most appropriately belong to the church. If so, the task of promoting a new and mutual discovery among the peoples of this earth is certainly the task of the church."[18]

The testimony of the other must be discovered and prioritized in the church as dialogical theology in order to provide both a witness against and an alternative to the racism and tribalism that permeate life in the world. For this vision to be fully realized, those who represent the hegemonic forms of theology that have served to marginalize the other in the church—as well as those in the schools and seminaries where so many traditional Christian leaders are trained—must accept and even embrace a particular challenge: the dominant theological traditions and intellectual assumptions of the Western church must be subjected to critical scrutiny and intentionally decentered in relation to other voices and traditions. This does not mean the Western church's traditions and assumptions are eclipsed, but only that they no longer occupy a normative position in the development and construction of missional theology. They take their place as particular manifestations of contextual theology. A particular challenge in this respect is that of whiteness and the assumptions of white supremacy.[19] This is because, in the words of James Cone, white people have been conditioned to think of themselves as "universal people" and consequently they "do not recognize the narrowness of their experience and the particularity of their theological expressions."[20] In this way they "fail to recognize that other people also have thought about

---

18. González, *Every Tribe and Nation*, 15.

19. See particularly Willie James Jennings, "Can White People Be Saved? Reflections on the Relationship of Missions and Whiteness," in *Can "White" People Be Saved? Triangulating Race, Theology, and Mission*, ed. Love L. Sechrest, Johnny Ramírez-Johnson, and Amos Yong, Missiological Engagements (Downers Grove, IL: IVP Academic, 2018), 27–43.

20. James H. Cone, *God of the Oppressed*, rev. ed. (Maryknoll, NY: Orbis, 1997), 13–14.

God and have something significant to say about Jesus' presence in the world."[21]

The culturally hegemonic and dominant traditions of theological discourse must assume a place at the ethnic roundtable along with all the other participants. These traditions must be willing to give up their assumption that they have theological and intellectual supremacy, and be prepared to listen rather than to speak—to assume the posture of a learner rather than that of a teacher. In so doing, Christians in these traditions will be in a position to receive the witness of the other and be liberated from the cultural imperialism that has deafened them to many voices and blinded them to the work of God.

Those who represent the dominant streams of theological reflection find this decentering especially challenging because of the power differential that exists between their own traditions and those outside of the dominant streams. In order to promote the Spirit-guided flourishing of God's intended plurality in the church, those with power must be willing to use that power to allow for the witness of the other in the life of the church, and they must also be willing to relinquish power for the sake of the gospel. This task of decentering will be difficult and often painful for those who have been formed and privileged by dominant Western theological traditions, but such a process is necessary for the witness of the church to the gospel of Jesus Christ. Thus for the sake of the gospel and the community that is called to bear living witness to it, we must in humility consider the interests and concerns of others before our own in keeping with the example of the Lord of the church, "who, though he was in the form of God, did not regard equality with God as something to be exploited, but emptied himself, taking the form of a slave" (Phil. 2:6–7).

That this is a matter of utmost importance for the witness of the gospel stems from the fact that the multiplicity of the church is

---

21. Cone, *God of the Oppressed*, 14.

not simply a fact; it is the very intention of God. Only a pluralist church and pluralist theology are able to bear appropriate witness to the kingdom intended by God. In light of this, González concludes that "the opposite of a pluralistic church and a pluralistic theology is not simply an exclusivistic church and a rigid theology, but a heretical church and a heretical theology!"[22]

One of the implications of the plurality that is an inherent part of the Word of God is the challenge that this entails for the traditional construal of theology as "systematic." This nomenclature suggests that theology can be conceived of as a relatively stable system of truth that is communicated in the act of revelation and that can be codified as a system of theology. It implies that the witness of Scripture may be summarized in the form of the system of theology that it supposedly contains and bears witness to. Now, without a doubt, the Bible has been read in such a fashion, with the result that numerous systems of theology have been discerned in its pages and proclaimed to be the one true system of doctrine taught in Scripture. Each such system then functions as an interpretive guideline for reading the Bible.

Missional theology offers an alternative to the assumptions of systematic theology. It does not proceed on the assumption that various genres and strands of the canon can be arranged into a uniform system of teaching, and therefore it does not suppress the plurality of the Bible and its witness to multiplicity revealed in the event of the Word of God. It takes into account not only the diversity of Scripture but also the diversity of the church throughout history as a manifestation of canonical plurality, as well as the plurality of social and historical situations in which Christian community comes to expression.

One of the dangers of the systematic approach to theology is that it quickly leads to sectarianism in the Christian community as different expressions of the church conclude that they have

22. González, *Every Tribe and Nation*, 25–26.

arrived at the one true system of doctrine. Inevitably they find themselves in conflict with other traditions that have reached different conclusions. The resulting fragmentation and divisiveness in the church is in clear contrast to the work of the Spirit in promoting the unity of the church. Yet how are we to account for the systematization that has characterized much of the Western theological tradition, particularly since the development of the scholasticism of the medieval church and the continuance of this approach to theology in the Protestant tradition? In other words, is systematization, with its challenges and dangers, inescapable in any theology that takes seriously its obligation to speak of God as a means of bearing witness to the truth of the gospel? Karl Barth addresses this question in a very helpful passage from the *Church Dogmatics* that is worth citing at length:

> In this work—it cannot be otherwise in view of its object—we have to do with the question of truth. It is, therefore, inevitable that as a whole and in detail the aim must be definiteness and coherence, and it is to be hoped that the definiteness and sequence of the truth will actually be disclosed. But this being the case, is it not also inevitable that "something like a system" will assert itself more or less spontaneously in dogmatic work? Why, then, should a "system" be so utterly abhorrent? If it asserts itself spontaneously in this way, can it not be forgiven? And if so, why should we be frightened away by a law forbidding systems? May it be that a "system" which asserts itself spontaneously (not as a system, but as a striving for definiteness and coherence) signifies obedience and is therefore a shadow of the truth? It may well be so. But even in this case the danger is still there. The fact that unauthorised systematisation may be forgiven does not mean that the tendency to systematisation is authorised. Nor does the fact that even in the fatal form of an intrinsically unauthorised systematisation true obedience may finally be demonstrated and a shadow of the truth disclosed.[23]

23. Karl Barth, *Church Dogmatics* 1/1, 868–69.

In other words, while the tendency of the discipline of theology to take on the form of systematic theology is understandable, perhaps even inevitable, the fact that it can disclose "a shadow of the truth" does not mean that it is ever to be seen as an authorized form of theology. Further, precisely because this systematic form of theology tends to assert itself spontaneously, we must vigilantly resist it through conscious and continual efforts. In response to this, missional theology takes on a particular set of commitments that serve to preserve the multiplicity and diversity inherent in the love and mission of God in the world.

The Shape of Missional Theology: Open and Committed to the Other

That love characterizes the mission of God from all eternity is the compelling basis for the extension of the divine mission to the world and gives distinctive shape to missional theology. In keeping with the centrality of love and relationality in the divine life, missional theology is open and committed to the other. It asserts that meaning and truth are not static entities that situated human beings can easily grasp and assimilate. Truth is not something that can be taken to the bank, deposited, and secured forevermore. Attempts to make truth absolute can reify it, as though it were a commodity that human beings can easily access and control, with the constant danger that it will then be put to use in ways that empower its holders at the expense of others. Instead, truth is a reality to which we must continually aspire. From the perspective of missional theology, this journey involves the commitment of our entire being to the love of God revealed in Jesus Christ through the power of the Spirit. It is a reality that constantly calls on us to privilege others above ourselves in accordance with the teaching and example of Jesus. It continually reminds us that we are always in a position of dependence and in need of grace with respect to our knowledge of God, who is the source of all truth.

The failure of humans to acknowledge our dependence on God and the ways in which we are prone to error has been common throughout history and inevitably leads to forms of oppression and conceptual idolatry.

In the Christian tradition, we are invited to see Jesus in the faces of others, particularly the poor and marginalized, and also to see God in Jesus. In this context, Jesus becomes the focal point for a theological orientation toward the other. The emphasis on the other and the complementary notion of hybridity are particularly promising aspects of postmodern thought that have great significance for the practice of missional theology. Among the connotations associated with the idea of otherness are philosophical, ethical, and eschatological concerns. In broadest terms, the other is viewed as anything or anyone that falls outside one's own categories. Here the realm and context of a person's own particular self (or what we might call "the same") is constantly confronted and pierced by that which is other, that which cannot be confined within the categories of the same. The challenge with respect to this aspect of otherness is to refrain from violating it by reducing it to the self-enclosed realm of the same, which would thereby force it into a homogenous, self-made mold that would efface it and eliminate its distinctive difference, its very otherness in relation to the same.[24] This has significance for the knowledge of God made known in the face of the other which cannot be thematized or conceptualized, suppressed or possessed. Instead, in the face of the other, in the very difference and strangeness of the other, the ultimate irreducibility of the other to sameness, we glimpse something of the epiphany of transcendence.[25]

24. For a seminal treatment of these ideas, see Edward Said, *Orientalism* (New York: Vintage, 1978).

25. For an extended treatment of the concepts of otherness and transcendence, see Emmanuel Levinas, *Alterity and Transcendence*, trans. M. Smith (New York: Columbia University Press, 1999).

Connected with openness to being nurtured by the other is the concept of *hybridity*, which represents the persistence of difference in unity. This is not the same as syncretism, which entails the attempt to unite opposing principles. Hybridity stands for resistance to hardened differences based on binary oppositions and the refusal to absorb all difference into a hegemonic notion of sameness. At its core, in order to celebrate difference and diversity, the postmodernist movement resists the totalizing power of reason. Missional theology shares this commitment. The agenda of openness to the other leads to a commitment to preserving the multiplicity of Christian witness that is an inherent part of the revelation of God's love in the world.

This accounts for the wide array of disparate discourses that share a commitment to postmodern thought. Reformed theologian James Olthuis summarizes this commitment admirably: "Ethically, postmodern discourses share an alertness to plurality and a vigilance on behalf of the other. Modernist rational ethics, in its Enlightenment dream of a world increasingly controlled by a pure rationality, has shown itself not only blind and indifferent to those who are other and different, those who fall outside the dominant discourse, but violent and oppressive to them."[26] Missional theology resists the totalizing power of reason in order to celebrate difference and diversity as a means of remaining open and committed to the witness of others.

Forms of theology that are properly shaped by the mission of God will continually be characterized by openness and commitment to the voices of others in the task of Christian witness. This is consistent with the rule of love that governs all forms of Christian discourse that would be faithful to the triune God of love who lives in eternal fellowship with otherness and difference. It is worthwhile to reiterate that the love of God does not seek

26. James Olthuis, "Face-to-Face: Ethical Asymmetry or the Symmetry of Mutuality?," in *Knowing Other-Wise: Philosophy at the Threshold of Spirituality*, ed. James Olthuis (New York: Fordham University Press, 1997), 135.

to assimilate the other. The emphasis on otherness in the life of the triune God as extended into the world through the revelation of God in Jesus Christ has great significance for the practice of theology. If we are to resist the dangers of cultural accommodation and come to know and bear witness to the fullness of the gospel, we must become open, and remain open, to the witness of others.

One of the ways in which openness and commitment to the voices of others bears on the practice of Christian theology is manifested in contexts where the dominance of a particular set of social and cultural assumptions and presuppositions has served to stamp the Bible and theology in its image. When this occurs, the voices of those who do not participate in the assumptions and presuppositions of the majority are marginalized or eclipsed, often under the guise of claims that they are not being faithful to Scripture or the Christian tradition by seeking to import a particular cultural agenda into the discipline of theology. Cultural imperialism is one of the great dangers in theology and easily leads to the suppression of voices that do not fit the accepted cultural norms for the practice of theology.

Openness to the plurality and difference of others calls on us to recognize the limitations of our own perspectives and experiences. It also invites us to live our lives for the sake of others as the means by which we can be delivered from the prison of our own imaginations and begin to experience something of the reality made known by God in Jesus Christ. This reality exceeds our particular language, thought-forms, and experiences, but from the perspective of the Christian biblical tradition it has come near to us in the person of Jesus Christ, who is the embodiment of the Way, the Truth, and the Life.

A posture of openness and commitment to others, the companion notion of hybridity, and a corresponding commitment to plurality for the sake of faithful Christian witness form the positive agenda of missional theology. In order to affirm and buttress this positive agenda, missional theology is also shaped by two closely related formal concerns whose function is to clear space for the flourishing of this agenda in the form of a community that is truly open and committed to others for the sake of the gospel and the sake of the world: it is beyond foundations and against totality.

The Shape of Missional Theology: Beyond Foundations

In keeping with its commitment to otherness, contextuality, and plurality, missional theology affirms the postmodern critique of strong or classic foundationalism.[27] The Enlightenment quest for epistemological certitude deeply shaped the modern era through the rejection of premodern notions of authority and replaced them with the notion of indubitable beliefs that are accessible to all individuals. Philosophically, foundationalism is a theory concerned with the justification of knowledge. It maintains that beliefs must be justified by their relationship to other beliefs and that the chain of justifications that results from this procedure must not be circular or endless, but must have a terminus in foundational beliefs that are immune from criticism and cannot be called into question. The goal of indubitable foundations is to attain a universal knowledge that transcends time and context. In keeping with this pursuit, the ideals of human knowledge since the Enlightenment have tended to focus on the universal, the general, and the theoretical rather than on the local, the particular, and the practical.

This conception of knowledge came to dominate the discipline of theology as theologians reshaped their conceptions of the Christian faith in accordance with its dictates. In the nineteenth and twentieth centuries, the foundationalist impulse produced a theological division between the left and the right. Liberals constructed theology upon the foundation of an unassailable religious experience, while conservatives looked to an error-free Bible as

27. For an extended discussion on the profile of a nonfoundational theology, see Stanley J. Grenz and John R. Franke, *Beyond Foundationalism: Shaping Theology in a Postmodern Context* (Louisville: Westminster John Knox, 2001).

the incontrovertible foundation of their theology.[28] It is interesting
to note that, for all their differences, both groups were drawing
from commonly held foundationalist conceptions of knowledge.
In other words, liberal and conservative theologians can often be
viewed as working out theological details from two different sides
of the same modernist, foundationalist coin.

Postmodern thought raises two related but distinct questions
about the modern foundationalist enterprise. First, is such an
approach to knowledge possible? And second, is it desirable?
These questions are connected with what may be viewed as the
two major branches of postmodern hermeneutical philosophy:
the hermeneutics of finitude and the hermeneutics of suspicion.
However, the challenges to foundationalism not only are philosophical but also emerge from the context of Christian theology.
Merold Westphal suggests that postmodern theory, with respect
to hermeneutical philosophy, may be properly appropriated for the
task of explicitly Christian thought on theological grounds: "The
hermeneutics of finitude is a meditation on the meaning of human
createdness, and the hermeneutics of suspicion is a meditation on
the meaning of human fallenness."[29] Viewed from this perspective, the questions raised by postmodern thought concerning the
possibility and desirability of foundationalism are also questions
that emerge from the material content of Christian theology. They
both lead to similar conclusions.

First, modern foundationalism is an impossible dream for finite
human beings whose outlooks are always limited and shaped by the
particular contexts from which they emerge. Second, the modern
foundationalist emphasis on the inherent goodness of knowledge
is shattered by the fallen and sinful nature of human beings who

28. On the liberal-conservative divide concerning the proper foundation for
theology, see Nancey Murphy, *Beyond Liberalism and Fundamentalism: How Modern and Postmodern Philosophy Set the Theological Agenda* (Valley Forge, PA: Trinity
Press International, 1996), 11–35.
29. Westphal, *Overcoming Onto-theology*, xx.

desire to seize control of the epistemic process in order to empower themselves and further their own ends, often at the expense of others. The limitations of finitude and the flawed condition of human nature mean that epistemic foundationalism is neither possible nor desirable for created and sinful persons. This double critique of foundationalism, emerging as it does from the perspectives of both postmodern philosophy and Christian theology, suggests the appropriateness and suitability, given the current intellectual situation, of the language of nonfoundationalism, which describes a postmodern, missional approach to the task of theology.

One of the most significant elements of nonfoundationalism for missional theology is its inherent commitment to contextuality, which requires the opening of theological conversation to the voices of persons and communities who have often been excluded from Western theological discourse. Nonfoundational epistemology, intercultural hermeneutics, and missional theology all maintain without reservation that no single human perspective, be it that of an individual or a particular community or theological tradition, is adequate to do full justice to the truth of God's revelation in Christ. Richard Mouw points to this issue as one of his own motivations for reflecting seriously about postmodern themes: "As many Christians from other parts of the world challenge our 'North Atlantic' theologies, they too ask us to think critically about our own cultural location, as well as about how we have sometimes blurred the boundaries between what is essential to the Christian message and the doctrine and frameworks we have borrowed from various Western philosophical traditions."[30] The adoption of a nonfoundationalist, intercultural, and missional approach to theology mandates a critical awareness of the role of culture and social location in the process of theological interpretation and construction.

---

30. Richard Mouw, "Delete the 'Post' from 'Postconservative,'" *Books & Culture* 7, no. 3 (May/June 2001): 22.

This nonfoundational approach to theology places emphasis on the local, the particular, and the practical rather than on the universal, the general, and the theoretical. According to William Stacy Johnson, nonfoundationalist theologies "share a common goal of putting aside all appeals to presumed self-evident, non-inferential, or incorrigible grounds for their intellectual claims."[31] They reject the notion that, among the many beliefs that make up a particular theology, there must be a single irrefutable foundation that is immune to criticism and provides the certain basis upon which all other assertions are founded. In nonfoundationalist theology, all beliefs are open to criticism and reconstruction. This does not mean, as is sometimes alleged, that nonfoundational theology cannot make assertions or maintain strong convictions that may be vigorously defended. As Francis Schüssler Fiorenza notes, to engage in nonfoundationalist theology is to accept that "it is a self-correcting enterprise that examines all claims, all relevant background theories."[32] Nonfoundationalist theology does not eschew convictions; it simply maintains that even the most long-standing and dear convictions are subject to critical scrutiny and potentially to revision, reconstruction, or even rejection. A missional theology beyond foundations seeks to respond positively and appropriately to the situatedness of all human thought and therefore to embrace a principled theological pluralism. It affirms that the ultimate authority in the church is not a particular source—Scripture, tradition, or culture—but only the living God revealed in Jesus Christ. This means that human beings are always in a position of dependence and in need of grace with respect to epistemic relations with God. Human attempts to seize control of these relations have been all too common throughout the history of the church and, no matter how well intentioned, inevitably lead to

31. William Stacy Johnson, *The Mystery of God: Karl Barth and the Postmodern Foundations of Theology* (Louisville: Westminster John Knox, 1997), 3.
32. Francis Schüssler Fiorenza, *Foundational Theology: Jesus and the Church* (New York: Crossroad, 1986), 287.

forms of conceptual idolatry and oppression. Missional theology seeks to nurture an open and flexible approach that is in keeping with the local, contextual character of human knowledge.

The Shape of Missional Theology: Against Totality

A third aspect of missional theology is closely related to the second. The commitment to resist foundationalism leads to a posture that is against totality. Because missional theology is committed to the radical contextuality of intercultural hermeneutics, it stands in opposition to claims that any particular theology is universal for all times and places. This commitment arises from both cultural-anthropological and missiological considerations. From the perspective of cultural anthropology, this stance against totality is connected to the sociology of knowledge and the linguistic turn. Anthropologists maintain that humans do not view the world from an objective vantage point but structure their world through the concepts they bring to it, particularly language. Human languages function as social conventions that describe the world in a variety of ways depending on the context of the speaker. Language constitutes the world in which we live and structures our perception of reality. However, no simple, one-to-one relationship exists between language and the world, and thus no single linguistic description can provide an objective conception of the so-called "real" world.

Anthropologists have discarded the older assumption that culture is a preexisting social-ordering force that is transmitted externally to members of a cultural group who in turn passively internalize it. They maintain that this view is mistaken in that it isolates culture from the ongoing social processes that produce and continually alter it. Culture is not an entity standing above or beyond human products and learned mental structures. In short, culture is not a thing.[33] The

33. Roy G. D'Andrade, *The Development of Cognitive Anthropology* (Cambridge: Cambridge University Press, 1995), 250.

modern understanding of culture as that which integrates the various
institutional expressions of social life and binds the individual to
society also faces serious challenges. According to Anthony Cohen,
it has become one of the casualties of the demise of "modernistic
grand theories and the advent of 'the interpretive turn' in its various
guises."[34]

Rather than exercising determinative power over people, culture
is conceived as the outcome and product of social interaction. In
this framework, human beings are not passive receivers; they are
active creators of culture.[35] Clifford Geertz provided the impetus
for this direction through his description of cultures as comprising
"webs of significance" that people spin and in which they are then
suspended.[36] Geertz defines culture as a "historically transmitted
pattern of meanings embodied in symbols, a system of inherited
conceptions expressed in symbolic forms by means of which people
communicate, perpetuate, and develop their knowledge about and
attitudes toward life."[37] According to Cohen, Geertz was responsible
for "shifting the anthropological view of culture from its supposedly
objective manifestations in social structures, towards its subjective
realisation by members who compose those structures."[38]

Culture resides in a set of meaningful forms and symbols
that, from the point of view of any particular individual, appear
as largely given.[39] Yet these forms are meaningful only because
human minds have the ability to interpret them. Anthropologists
look at the interplay of cultural artifacts and human interpretation
in the formation of meaning. They suggest that, contrary to the
belief that meaning lies in signs or in the relations between them,

34. Anthony P. Cohen, *Self Consciousness: An Alternative Anthropology of Identity* (London: Routledge, 1994), 118.
35. Cohen, *Self Consciousness*, 118–19.
36. Clifford Geertz, *The Interpretation of Cultures* (New York: Basic Books, 1973), 5.
37. Geertz, *Interpretation of Cultures*, 89.
38. Cohen, *Self Consciousness*, 135.
39. Geertz, *Interpretation of Cultures*, 45.

meanings are bestowed by the users of signs. However, this does not mean that individuals simply discover or make up cultural meanings on their own. The thrust of contemporary cultural anthropology lies in understanding the creation of cultural meaning as connected to world construction and identity formation.

This approach leads to an understanding of culture as socially constructed. The thesis of social constructionists such as Peter Berger is that we do not inhabit a prefabricated, given world; we live in a linguistically construed social-cultural world of our own creation. At the heart of the process whereby we construct our world is the imposition of some semblance of a meaningful order upon our variegated experiences.[40] For the interpretive framework we employ, we are dependent on the society in which we participate.[41] Society mediates to us the cultural tools necessary for constructing our world.

Although this constructed world seems to be a universal and objective reality, it is actually, in the words of David Morgan, "an unstable edifice that generations constantly labor to build, raze, rebuild, and redesign."[42] We inhabit linguistically and socially constructed worlds to which our personal identities are intricately bound. The construction of these worlds and the formation of personal identity are ongoing, dynamic, and fluid processes in which the forming and reforming of shared cultural meanings play a crucial role. To be human is to be embedded in culture. In numerous conversations that shape our ever-shifting contexts, we participate in the process of interpretation and the creation of meaning as we reflect on and internalize the cultural symbols that we share with others.

The situated, contextual character of all human discourse leads missiologist Andrew Walls to affirm what he calls the "indigenizing

40. Peter L. Berger, *The Sacred Canopy: Elements of a Sociological Theory of Religion* (Garden City, NY: Doubleday, 1967), 3–13.
41. Berger, *Sacred Canopy*, 20.
42. David Morgan, *Visual Piety: A History and Theory of Popular Images* (Berkeley: University of California Press, 1998), 9.

principle" as a central element of the very substance of the gospel.[43] The indigenizing principle is rooted in the core gospel affirmation that God comes to us where we are and accepts us through the work of Christ—not on the basis of what we have been, are, or are trying to become. This acceptance of us as we are points to the notion that God does not relate to us as isolated, self-sufficient individuals but rather as people who are conditioned by the particular times, places, families, societies, groups, and cultures in which we live. In Christ we are accepted by God in the midst of all the relations, experiences, and cultural conditioning that make us who we are.

The notion of being a new creation in Christ is not intended to suggest that a convert to the way of Jesus starts a new life in a vacuum with a mind that becomes a blank slate. We are all formed by our social, cultural, and historical circumstances. The affirmation that God has accepted us as we are means that our lives and minds will continue to be influenced by ways in which they have been developed along with the assumptions and presuppositions that we have learned. These are not somehow eliminated from our consciousness; they continue to shape the ways in which we view the world. It is also worth noting that this reality is "as true for groups as for persons. All churches are culture churches—including our own."[44]

The plurality of the church is a faithful expression of the plurality of Scripture, which is in turn a faithful witness to the plurality of truth lived out in the eternal life of God and expressed in the act of revelation. Plurality is the intention and will of God as a faithful expression of truth. In the words of Lamin Sanneh, "For most of us it is difficult enough to respect those with whom we might disagree, to say nothing of those who might be different from us in culture, language, and tradition. For all of us pluralism can be a rock of stumbling, but for God it is the cornerstone of the universal design."[45]

43. Walls, *Missionary Movement*, 3–9.
44. Walls, *Missionary Movement*, 8.
45. Sanneh, *Translating the Message*, 27.

CHAPTER

5

Missional Solidarity

As we explore the multiplicity and manifold witness of the Christian community in its witness to the gospel and the kingdom of God, readers might well be wondering about the unity of the church. If the witness of the church is—must be—characterized by plurality and multiplicity, how are we to understand the unity that Scripture calls us to manifest and preserve? How can we conceive of the unity of the Christian community in the midst of a pluralist church that throughout history and across cultures has been embodied in such a dazzling array of forms? Is unity attainable when so much is debated and contested with respect to beliefs and practices? While Christians around the world confess that they believe in one, holy, catholic, and apostolic church, does not the simple fact of Christian diversity force us to ask, Is the church really one? And if it is, how are we to understand this unity in the midst of its sheer and irreducible plurality? In what sense, if any, may the diverse global Christian communities of the past and the diverse global Christian communities of the present be said to somehow be "one" with each other?

We might first consider why such questions even matter. Do Christians have any stake in affirming the unity of the church, or must it be that the competing practices and traditions of the church will cause us to move forward in a sectarian fashion, with each community sure that it represents the one truth? Sadly, the latter often has appeared to be the case for Christians from across the ideological spectrum. The diversity of the Christian community has been the basis for disunity and even hostility between churches as they struggle to assert their claims of primacy and greater faithfulness. However, such an exclusivist understanding of church and theology is contrary to the mission and intentions of God in the witness of the New Testament, which calls the church to live in harmony and relates this unity to its witness to the gospel.

Unity/Solidarity

In the midst of bearing witness to the polyphonic (many voiced) character of the one faith, Scripture also extols the concept of unity or solidarity. A commitment to plurality and difference allows for a healthy freedom of expression that is important for true harmony. But one of the great dangers of the freedom engendered by plurality is that it easily becomes the basis for discord and hostility as each asserts their freedom over against others. Paul warns about this in his letter to the churches in Galatia: "For you were called to freedom, brothers and sisters; only do not use your freedom as an opportunity for self-indulgence, but through love become slaves to one another. For the whole law is summed up in a single commandment, 'You shall love your neighbor as yourself.' If, however, you bite and devour one another, take care that you are not consumed by one another" (Gal. 5:13–15).

In response to the danger that plurality and freedom might lead to strife and violence, both the Hebrew Bible and the New Testament promote the goodness and importance of unity. Psalm

133 is a classic expression of unity: "How very good and pleasant it is when kindred live together in unity!" (v. 1). This assertion is illustrated in two ways consistent with Hebrew parallelism: through references to the anointing of Aaron (v. 2) and the dew of Mount Hermon (v. 3). Both of these illustrations feature liquids: anointing oil and dew.

First, unity is "like the precious oil on the head, running down upon the beard, on the beard of Aaron, running down over the collar of his robes" (v. 2). The reference to Aaron makes it clear that the oil referred to here is the fragrant, refreshing oil used to consecrate a Hebrew priest. This oil is precious—consisting of olive oil, liquid myrrh, and cinnamon among other spices—and fills the air with a sweet, pleasing aroma that signifies the pleasantness of life as it is intended by God. We can close our eyes and imagine this wonderful aroma in the contemporary setting: freshly brewed coffee in the morning; a stuffed turkey roasting in the oven on Thanksgiving or Christmas; freshly baked pies and treats cooling in the kitchen. That is what unity is like: a pleasing sweet aroma that fills the air and signifies worship, feasting, and celebration.

Second, unity is "like the dew of Hermon, which falls on the mountains of Zion" (v. 3). Mount Hermon is well to the north of Jerusalem (aka Zion) and is the highest mountain in Israel. Its moisture runs into rivulets that flow into the Jordan River, which runs north to south through Israel, irrigating and giving life to arid lands where infrequent rains lead to dry riverbeds and a lack of water. This scarcity of water in a dry land makes the dews of Mount Hermon so precious. That is what unity is like: it travels far beyond its point of origin and gives life to distant lands.

The ancient readers of this psalm would have understood the allusion to the flowing of oil and dew down from Aaron's beard and the slopes of Mount Hermon to bring sweetness and life-giving abundance to those around them. This is a "Song of Ascent," one of the fifteen psalms (Pss. 120–134) that start with that ascription.

Many scholars believe the title indicates that these psalms were sung by worshipers as they ascended the road to Jerusalem and the Temple Mount. Others have suggested that Levitical priests sang these psalms as they ascended the steps to minister in the temple. In either case, ancient readers would not have missed the significance of unity in worship flowing down from the Jerusalem temple to bring goodness and life to the surrounding lands, and indeed all the earth. Think of the similarity with the promise of Jesus to his disciples at the beginning of Acts: "You will be my witnesses in Jerusalem, in all Judea and Samaria, and to the ends of the earth" (1:8). As the message of the gospel proclaimed by the followers of Jesus produces unity and peace, it will bring goodness and life to all the earth.

This is consistent with the covenant God made with Abraham—that his people would be a blessing to the nations. In the midst of a world torn asunder by discord, God calls a people to tell a different story and live an alternative life, a life in which the social conventions that divide people from each other—race, ethnicity, gender, social/economic class, sexual orientation, political preferences, ideologies, and any other construction that human beings can invent to suggest that some people are inferior and unworthy of God's blessing—are set aside for a vision of unity in the midst of diversity and difference. One faith is expressed in many voices committed to unity for the sake of the world.

This is God's vision for the world—a peaceful and harmonious community in which everyone has enough and no one needs to be afraid. It is for this reason that the New Testament is so concerned with the unity of the church.

Perhaps the most significant text in the New Testament concerning the unity of the church is found in John 17. John reports that after Jesus prays that his disciples would be sanctified in truth by the Word of God, which is truth itself, he affirms that he is sending them into the world as he himself had been sent. Then, turning his attention to the unity of the church, Jesus prays for

his disciples and the church, asking that they might all be one in
a way that is like the unity that he shares with the Father in order
that the world might believe he was sent by the Father:

> I ask not only on behalf of these, but also on behalf of those who
> will believe in me through their word, that they may all be one. As
> you, Father, are in me and I am in you, may they also be in us, so
> that the world may believe that you have sent me. The glory that
> you have given me I have given them, so that they may be one, as we
> are one, I in them and you in me, that they may become completely
> one, so that the world may know that you have sent me and have
> loved them even as you have loved me. (John 17:20–23)

Note the close connection made between the knowledge of the
truth, the sending of Jesus, and the unity of the church. Jesus is
sent into the world to be the light of the world, to forgive sin, and
to proclaim and demonstrate love and salvation in order that the
world might believe and follow in his way. Jesus has entrusted
the church with the continuance of that mission as a community
sent into the world as a sign, instrument, and foretaste of the
reign of God, bearing witness to the reality that Jesus was sent
by the Father for the purpose of reconciling the world to God.
The unity for which Jesus prays is to be a prime indicator of this
truth, "that they may become completely one, so that the world
may know that you have sent me." In other words, the oneness is
to be demonstrable so that it can actually be seen by the world as
a visible testimony to the reconciling love of God in Jesus Christ.
This indicates that the unity of the church is vitally connected
with its life and witness and is a central aspect of its missional
vocation to be the people of God in the world.

This concern for visible unity is prominent in other parts of
the New Testament too. In the letter to the Ephesians, after an
exposition of the divine peace initiative reconciling the people
of the world, the church is called upon to adopt attitudes and

practices that will exemplify this reality and make it visible in the world. Unity is not simply an invisible reality but also a calling that is to be manifested in visible ways through the cultivation of the disciplines of humility, gentleness, patience, and forbearance with others. The letter to the Philippians draws connections between these qualities and the life of Jesus, who did not consider equality with God something to be grasped but instead humbled himself, taking the form of a servant. The letter urges the church to follow this example (Phil. 2:1–11). The letter to the Galatians speaks of these qualities of love, joy, peace, patience, kindness, goodness, faithfulness, gentleness, and self-control as the fruit of the Spirit against which there is no law (Gal. 5:22–26). God calls the church to a complete and visible oneness like that which the Father shares with the Son.

It is ironic, given the close connection between the belief that the Father sent the Son to redeem the world and the unity of the church, that one of the most significant challenges to the unity of the church comes from those who make certain kinds of truth claims. The letter to Titus addresses this in an explicit warning against divisiveness in the church of Jesus Christ: "But avoid stupid controversies, genealogies, dissensions, and quarrels about the law, for they are unprofitable and worthless. After a first and second admonition, have nothing more to do with anyone who causes divisions, since you know that such a person is perverted and sinful, being self-condemned" (3:9–11). Now, doubtless, those who want to argue about such things do so under the guise of truth. They say that we must all believe and maintain their particular conception of the law because it is the one proper understanding. They are convinced that it is the one and only truth, and on that basis they foster discord and dissension in the church in pursuit of their own views and interests. We could easily add the word *theology* to this passage with no distortion of meaning. Some debates that have become controversies in the church are simply not profitable. They needlessly divide the church and distract it from its missional vocation. The prescriptions offered in the letter are clear: warn twice those who are divisive and then have nothing to do with them because they are not committed to the unity of the church.

Clearly, according to the witness of Scripture and in keeping with the prayer of Jesus, the unity of the church is a matter of utmost importance that the Spirit is jealous to protect and that the members of the community are called upon to preserve and promote. These texts point to the importance of the visible unity of the church as a testimony to the world of the truth of the gospel. As such, the church is called upon to make every effort to preserve the unity of the Spirit and to vigilantly oppose those who promote division in the church. The promotion and preservation of the unity of the church is part of its missional vocation. The mission of the church is vitally connected with an appropriate and visible manifestation of its unity in the midst of its diversity, and failure to maintain this unity will significantly compromise its mission and witness to the world.

If we fail at this point, no matter how right we may be regarding anything else we believe, we fail. Hence, the opening words of Ephesians 4: "I therefore, the prisoner in the Lord, beg you to lead a life worthy of the calling to which you have been called, with all humility and gentleness, with patience, bearing with one another in love, making every effort to maintain the unity of the Spirit in the bond of peace. There is one body and one Spirit, just as you were called to the one hope of your calling, one Lord, one faith, one baptism, one God and Father of all, who is above all and through all and in all" (4:1–6).

This is a reminder that while we cannot control those around us, we can commit to make every effort to maintain the unity of the Spirit by cultivating the disciplines of humility, gentleness, patience, and forbearance in our lives. As each of us does this, together among our families, friends, colleagues, fellow church members, and those we meet along life's pathways, we

will experience not only how very good and pleasant it is when
kindred live together in unity but also what the psalmist identifies
as the blessing of the Lord: "life forevermore" (Ps. 133:3). Missional theology works to promote the solidarity of the church
through the articulation and cultivation of ideas and practices
that result in the characteristics of discipleship called for by
Jesus. The unity of the church is preserved not by doctrinal or
theological uniformity or agreement but by the development of
personal and communal formation consistent with the kingdom
of God proclaimed by Jesus.

Solidarity and Multiplicity

Part of the challenge in maintaining visible unity among Christian
communities stems from the pervasive individualism in society
that leads not only to personal individualism and the notion of
the autonomous self but also to a sectarian individualism with
respect to the church. This occurs when we come to think that
our particular church or tradition is the sole bearer of truth and
the only proper way to bear witness to the gospel. Such notions
are the products of individualistic ecclesiologies that fail to comprehend the interconnectedness of the whole church as the one
body of Christ in the world, even in the diversity of its expression.

Theology that serves the church in ways that are consonant
with its missional vocation must seek to promote and preserve
the unity of the church in accordance with the work of the Spirit
and the witness of Scripture. Missional theology seeks to develop
constructions and formulations of Christian faith that promote
and maintain the unity of the church and the interconnectedness
and solidarity that are called forth by the metaphor of the church
as the body of Christ in the world, which is not divided but is
one. Interconnectedness and solidarity between churches remind
us of the dual responsibilities involved in the missional calling
of the church: to bear local witness to the gospel in the context

of particular social, cultural, and historical circumstances while remaining faithful to the whole church in its historical and global expressions.

It needs to be added that, while the one faith takes on multiple expressions, not all expressions of the one faith are appropriate. Some are problematic, which is why a critical aspect of missional theology is the ongoing process of assessing the church's proclamation and practices (as discussed in chap. 3). The unity of the church is not to be sought merely as an end in itself but rather as a unity centered on the truth of the gospel and the Word of God as it is worked out in mission to the world.

The sort of unity often imagined is that of a church in agreement around a universal theology or the practice of a common liturgy or shared understanding of the proper principles of biblical interpretation. Much ecumenical conversation has been pursued in the past in order to arrive at a common confession and theology through the incorporation of various insights, and the rejection of others, into a melting pot out of which it is hoped will emerge a singular expression of Christian faith, thereby securing the unity of the church. It is also suggested, implicitly by some and explicitly by others, that the church cannot manifest this unity apart from a common theological expression of this sort, since that would amount to a compromise of truth. The danger here is equating unity with uniformity.

In the expression of missional theology developed in this book, there is a different conception of unity, one that not only affirms the value of multiplicity but also connects it directly with the mission of God as a necessary component of living God's love in the world. From this perspective, we should not expect complete agreement and commonality on matters of theology and biblical interpretation. If this is the case, where is the unity of the church to be found in a pluralist church with a pluralist theology?

In order to engage this situation and the challenges it poses for the solidarity of the Christian tradition, missiologist Andrew

Walls raises a provocative question: Is there in fact a historic
Christian faith? To illustrate the pluriform character of the tradition and raise questions about unity and solidarity, he offers
an instructive and clever example.[1] He invites us to imagine
a long-living, scholarly space visitor, perhaps a "Professor of
Comparative Inter-Planetary Religions" who visits Earth every
few centuries in order to study Christianity. On the first trip to
Earth, our space scholar visits the original Jerusalem Christians,
who are all Jews and who practice Judaism from the perspective
of the teachings of Jesus of Nazareth. They meet in the temple,
offer animal sacrifices, scrupulously refrain from all work on the
seventh day of the week, circumcise their male children, regularly perform certain rituals, and carefully read and follow the
teaching of the law and the prophets contained in the Hebrew
Scriptures. Unlike other Jews, however, they identify Jesus as
the Messiah, Son of Man, and Suffering Servant described in
those Scriptures.

During the next visit, our scholar attends the Council of Nicaea
in 325. Those at this meeting are unmarried men who come from
many different geographical areas around the Mediterranean, and
none of them are Jewish—in fact, some refer to Jews in very hos-
tile terms. They connect "sacrifice" with bread and wine rather
than animals, and they refuse to circumcise male children. They
worship on the first day of the week instead of the seventh. Although they read a translation of the law books used by the Jerusalem Christians, they also value writings that were not even in
existence during the scholar's first visit to Jerusalem. They also
seem concerned with giving precise definitions to certain philosophical and theological words such as *homoousios* ("one being")
and usually refer to Jesus as Son of God or Lord rather than Son
of Man or Suffering Servant.

1. Andrew F. Walls, *The Missionary Movement in Christian History: Studies in
the Transmission of Faith* (Maryknoll, NY: Orbis, 1996), 3–7.

Three centuries later, the scholar visits Ireland and finds Christian monks pursuing lives of holiness by standing in freezing water and reciting psalms, praying in relative isolation from others, and performing bizarre acts of penance. Groups of these monks also risk their lives on long journeys, attempting to convince others to worship Jesus as God rather than nature gods. They write and illustrate beautiful manuscripts of the same sacred texts used at the Council of Nicaea and seem to put a great deal of emphasis on determining the correct date of Easter. They recite the creed developed at the Council, but they do not have the same philosophical or theological interests.

In the 1840s the professor visits a Christian assembly in London, where the speakers are promoting missionary and commercial efforts in Africa as well as the abolition of slavery. Many at the meeting have their own English translation of the books used by the earlier Christians, but they do not appear to live in the same degree of poverty. Like the monks, they emphasize holiness, but they utterly reject the idea that holiness has anything to do with standing in cold water or living in isolation from others.

The final visit is to Lagos, Nigeria, in the late twentieth century, where people wearing white robes dance and chant in the street on their way to church. They say that they experience the power of God in their services through healing and the reception of specific messages from God. They are quite removed from the London assembly's way of life, and while they fast like the Irish, they do so only on certain occasions. They use the same sacred text as the London group, but they are focused on the power that comes from preaching, miraculous physical healing, and personal visions.

In exploring this multiplicity, Walls asks what conclusions can be drawn from the observations concerning the diverse communities, beliefs, and practices that constitute historic Christianity. "It is not simply that these five groups of humans, all claiming to be Christians, appear to be concerned about different things;

the concerns of one group appear suspect or even repellent to another."[2] Can any coherence be found among the diverse communities mentioned? Can one reasonably maintain that these varied groups were all participants in an identifiable religious tradition beyond the mere fact that they all considered themselves to be Christian and shared this common name? Walls answers in the affirmative and mentions two aspects that have shaped the common Christian tradition. The first is the "historical connection," while the second is an "essential continuity" that exists between the groups mentioned.

Regarding the historical connection, Jewish Christians took the gospel to Greek gentiles. The classical Greek or Hellenistic culture in which these gentile Christians lived shaped the conception of Christianity that became dominant in the Roman Empire. With the collapse of the Roman world and its institutions and intellectual traditions, Christianity continued on in Ireland, whose monks evangelized Europe. In turn, the European evangelization of the world shaped the most recent phase of Christianity, the emergence of the world church. While this history of mission and evangelization is characterized by failure and tragedy as well as by the transmission of the gospel, it does point to the common theme of mission among these communities and the abiding sense that they exist not simply to serve their own ends but for a purpose in the world related to the calling and intentions of the God made known in Jesus. The Christian community "continues as church as it continues Jesus' mission of preaching, serving and witnessing to God's already-inaugurated yet still-to-be-consummated reign, growing and changing and being transformed in the process."[3]

In addition to this historical and missional connection, Walls identifies an essential continuity. "There is, in all the wild profusion of the varying statements of these differing groups, one

2. Walls, *Missionary Movement*, 5.
3. Stephen B. Bevans and Roger P. Schroeder, *Constants in Context: A Theology of Mission for Today* (Maryknoll, NY: Orbis, 2004), 33.

theme which is as unvarying as the language which expresses it
is various; that the person of Jesus called the Christ has ultimate
significance."[4] In the midst of all its diversity and profusion, the
church experiences solidarity across time and space through its
commitment to Jesus. Walls also notes that all of the differing
groups make use of bread and wine and water in their ritual practices and that all the groups appeal to the same ancient texts,
though their interpretations of these writings vary considerably
and are often at odds with each other. "Still more remarkable is the
continuity of consciousness. Each group thinks of itself as having
some community with the others, so different in time and place,
and despite being so obviously out of sympathy with many of their
principal concerns."[5] He concludes that these realities reflect the
essential continuity of the plurality of communities and traditions
that make up the one Christian tradition, while acknowledging
"that these continuities are cloaked with such heavy veils belonging to their environment that Christians of different times and
places must often be unrecognizable to others, or indeed even to
themselves, as manifestations of a single phenomenon."[6] In ac-
counting for the staggering diversity of the Christian tradition,
Walls suggests that the history of Christianity has always been
a struggle between two opposing tendencies that have been part
of the missionary expansion of the church and its witness and
that find their basis in the very substance of the gospel itself. He
refers to these as the "indigenizing principle" and the "pilgrim
principle."[7]

As mentioned earlier, the *indigenizing principle* is rooted in the
gospel affirmation that God comes to us where we are and accepts
us through the work of Christ, not based on our past or present
realities. This acceptance indicates that God does not relate to us

4. Walls, *Missionary Movement*, 6.
5. Walls, *Missionary Movement*, 6–7.
6. Walls, *Missionary Movement*, 6–7.
7. Walls, *Missionary Movement*, 7–9.

as isolated individuals but as people who are shaped by the times and places in which we live, as well as by the particular families, societies, groups, and cultures in which we participate. In Christ we are accepted by God in the midst of all those contexts, experiences, and relationships that make us who we are. The impossibility of separating ourselves from our social relationships and the societies in which we belong leads to an unwavering commitment to indigenization—that is, to living life as both a Christian and as a member of a particular society, culture, and people group—that has been characteristic of the best in the Christian tradition.

The account of the Jerusalem Council in Acts 15 provides an affirmation of this principle of indigenization with the decision that gentiles should be permitted to enter into the faith without being bound to Jewish Christians' rituals and practices. The most significant of these decisions was the determination that male gentile converts would not need to undergo circumcision. The affirmation that God accepts people as they are means that those who have not participated in the past in such customs as circumcision, dietary restrictions, and ritual cleansings need not do so in order to be part of the community of Christ's disciples. In light of this, Walls asserts that no particular group of Christians "has therefore any right to impose in the name of Christ upon another group of Christians a set of assumptions about life determined by another time and place."[8] Every expression of Christian faith arises from a particular social setting that thoroughly shapes it, even as it attempts to express transcultural values.

In tension with the indigenizing principle is the *pilgrim* or *transformation principle*, which is also intimately connected with the gospel. While it is true that God meets people where they are and as they are, it is also true that the intention of the gospel is transformative. God in Christ calls us to be transformed by the power of the gospel and to participate in the mission of God in

8. Walls, *Missionary Movement*, 8.

the world. This call to transformation means that even in light of the indigenizing principle that affirms culture and experience, followers of Christ find that they are not completely in sync with their cultural and historical surroundings. The transformation principle reminds Christians that we will never be completely at home in this world and that we must always be seeking the renewal of our minds and lives and resisting conformity to many of the social and cultural patterns of our societies. In other words, faithfulness to Christ will often put us out of step with our culture.

While the indigenizing principle affirms that Christians remain appropriately related to the relationships and thought-forms in which they are raised and seek their renewal in Christ, the transformation principle points to an entirely new set of relations with others who are part of the community of Christ's disciples. These relations call on us to accept others and all of their group relations just as God has accepted them, while at the same time seeking the transformation of all things in Christ in accordance with the will and mission of God. All Christians have dual nationalities and loyalties to multiple Christian faith communities in Christ. These loyalties and commitments link us beyond our own affinity groups to individuals and their communities who are naturally opposed, by cultural and historical assumption and presupposition, to the very things to which we are committed. In addition to these relationships, Christians are given an adoptive past that links us to the people of God throughout all of history. In this way "all Christians of whatever nationality, are landed by adoption with several millennia of someone else's history, with a whole set of ideas, concepts, and assumptions which do not necessarily square with the rest of their cultural inheritance; and the Church in every land, of whatever race and type of society, has this same adoptive past by which it needs to interpret the fundamentals of the faith."[9]

9. Walls, *Missionary Movement*, 9.

These principles point to the complexity and plurality of the faith as it has been expressed throughout the history of the Christian tradition, and they point to our calling to take responsibility for this plurality in bearing witness to the gospel of Jesus Christ. They may also function as a basis for solidarity in the midst of missional multiplicity as the Christian community affirms the significance of culture in all articulations of the gospel, church, and theology.

Commenting on these conclusions, Stephen Bevans and Roger Schroeder speak of this essential continuity described by Walls as the means by which Christianity "remains itself as it transforms itself in missionary outreach. Despite differences of language, context, and culture, there persist as well certain *constants* that define Christianity in its missionary nature."[10] These can be summarized as being connected to the constants of Christology and ecclesiology. Christologically, Jesus of Nazareth is always at the center of these diverse communities and of ultimate significance. The intention to trust in him and follow him shapes the reason these communities exist. With respect to the church, Bevans and Schroeder note that in spite of Christian communities' differing notions of the significance of the Bible, how best to practice baptism and the Lord's Supper, and who they are in the world, they see themselves as communities "that are nourished and equipped" for their work in the world by both word and sacrament. Bevans and Schroeder conclude that, though the particular content of these constants is not the same, Christianity "is never without faith in and theology of Jesus as Christ and never without a commitment to and understanding of the community it names church."[11]

In addition to these two constants—the centrality of Jesus Christ and the ecclesial nature of Jesus's disciples in their missional activity (expressed in fidelity to a common book, a common

10. Bevans and Schroeder, *Constants in Context*, 33.
11. Bevans and Schroeder, *Constants in Context*, 33.

heritage, and a common ritual)—Bevans and Schroeder propose four more: eschatology, salvation, anthropology, and culture. They suggest that these concerns, and the questions and challenges they continually pose for communities committed to mission in the world, are all integral to an understanding of Christian faith that has shaped the life and witness of churches throughout history and across cultures. As such, they are constitutive of the unity of the church as a community gathering around the living presence of Jesus Christ in common mission grappling with common concerns. Christian solidarity is not to be found in set, uniform answers to these concerns but rather in the common questions they raise. "The answers to these questions about Jesus, the church, the future, salvation, and human nature and human culture have certainly varied through the two millennia of Christianity's existence, as the church has lived out its missionary nature in various contexts. As *questions*, however, they remain ever present and ever urgent, because how they are answered is how Christianity finds its concrete identity as it constitutes itself in fidelity to Jesus' mission."[12]

Here we see that the unity of the church throughout history and across culture can be discerned in its shared missional vocation as a community sent into the world by God through Jesus Christ in the power of the Spirit, and in its common theological and practical concerns as expressed in the sort of "essential continuity" or "constants in context" mentioned by Walls, Bevans, and Schroeder. These common connections provide a theological and practical basis for Christian solidarity in the past, the present, and the future as particular and diverse Christian communities participate together, in various ways, in one common mission, the mission of God.

C. S. Lewis has provided a very helpful way of thinking about the church along these lines in the opening pages of his classic

12. Bevans and Schroeder, *Constants in Context*, 34.

work *Mere Christianity*. To describe the church, he uses the metaphor of a house containing "a hall out of which doors open into several rooms." The hall represents what he calls "mere" Christianity, and the rooms represent the existing communions and traditions in the church. Lewis states that the goal of the book is to help readers find their way into the hall, but he also makes it clear that readers should not suppose that he is suggesting that "mere Christianity" is an alternative to the creeds, confessions, and practices of existing communions, as if one could simply choose it in preference to a particular community. For, as he puts it, "it is in the rooms, not in the hall, that there are fires and chairs and meals. The hall is a place to wait in, a place to try various doors, not a place to live in. For that purpose the worst of the rooms (whichever that may be) is, I think, preferable." In other words, while the hall serves the important function of providing the structure for Christian unity, the rooms are the places where the whole counsel of God is worked out in the social life and fabric of particular communities. The hall is not a place to live but rather a place to wait on the Lord for guidance in the process of finding a room and to begin to obey the rules common to the whole house. Above all, these rules require that "you must be asking which door is the true one; not which pleases you best by its paint and paneling. In plain language, the question should never be: 'Do I like that kind of service?' but 'Are these doctrines true: Is holiness here?'" He concludes by saying that once one has reached one's room, it is important to be kind to those who have chosen different doors. "If they are wrong they need your prayers all the more; and if they are your enemies, then you are under orders to pray for them. That is one of the rules common to the whole house."[13]

This metaphor of a house with many rooms provides a helpful way to conceptualize the multiplicity and unity of the church. It

13. C. S. Lewis, *Mere Christianity* (New York: Macmillan, 1952), 11–12.

pictures the church as bearing a diverse and contextual witness to the gospel that reflects the variety of perspectives contained in the biblical narratives, the variety of social and historical contexts in which the message of Scripture is received, and the different responses of particular human beings who view the world in richly different ways. These various communities are unified around the presence of Christ, a shared commitment to participate in his mission, a shared historical continuity, and a set of concerns and practices common to the whole house.

In the midst of this diversity, it is the living person of Jesus who is at the center animating the life of the whole Christian community through the ages, even while being experienced in rich and diverse ways. Each of these experiences, mediated by the Spirit, provides greater awareness and understanding of the ways in which Jesus is the Christ. "Jesus always remains the Christ, although his Christness—the way he is understood as of ultimate significance—is expressed differently and understood more deeply in the church's various historical and cultural embodiments."[14]

Missional Christology

It is important to make a distinction between the history of the church's comprehension of Christ, its Christology, and the actual living presence of Christ. Christology has a rich history of reflection in the tradition of the church, and it has spawned numerous constructive proposals based upon various elements of the witness of Scripture. However, the particular framing of these proposals may in fact have obscured points of solidarity in the church and led to unnecessary division. Two points stand out in this respect.

The first is the relative lack of engagement with the mission and life of Jesus as it is narrated in the Gospels. Discussion has tended to focus more on abstract questions concerned with intratrinitarian

14. Bevans and Schroeder, *Constants in Context*, 33.

relationships, the relationship between the divine and human natures of the person of Christ, and the atonement. The shape of this conversation can seem to suggest that the details of Jesus's life and ministry have little doctrinal significance for the major questions of Christology as they have been understood in the classical tradition. "As a rule, dogmatics has based itself on the proclamation structure of the epistles, not the story structure of the gospels."[15] This tendency also seems to situate theological discussions in a more abstract and intellectual context that often seems far removed from the day-to-day life of the witnessing community. This can give the impression that faithful Christianity is more about a set of correct beliefs than it is an alternative, concrete way of life. Such an approach to theology tends to privilege disembodied ideas over against an incarnational approach that is centered on lived theology.

Second, the intuitions of the classical tradition have been formed and developed almost exclusively in the context of Christendom. Lesslie Newbigin remarks that much "of the substance of the Western Christian tradition—its liturgy, theology and church order—was formed during the long period in which Western Christendom was an almost enclosed ghetto precluded from missionary advance."[16] In addition, the dominance of this tradition has retarded the reception and influence of the theological contributions of Christian communities from beyond the West and those that have been underrepresented in the structures and assumptions of hegemonic theological discourse. This has left the impression among many students of theology that Western forms of theology and Christology are more faithful to the interpretation of Scripture than are non-Western forms.

Philippians 2 speaks of imitating the way of Jesus in solidarity with him: being of the same mind, having the same love, being in

15. Hendrikus Berkhof, *Christian Faith: An Introduction to the Study of Faith* (Grand Rapids: Eerdmans, 1979), 293.
16. Lesslie Newbigin, *The Open Secret: An Introduction to the Theology of Mission*, rev. ed. (Grand Rapids: Eerdmans, 1995), 4.

full accord and of one mind with Jesus such that we do nothing from selfish ambition but rather in humility regard others as better than ourselves. We are called to look to the interests of others rather than our own and to be intentional about engaging the world for the sake of its transformation into the world intended by God. The unity of the church is found in its imitation and solidarity with Jesus, "who, though he was in the form of God, did not regard equality with God as something to be exploited, but emptied himself, taking the form of a slave, being born in human likeness. And being found in human form, he humbled himself and became obedient to the point of death—even death on a cross" (Phil. 2:6–8).

The way of Jesus is not simply about the inwardly focused or otherworldly spirituality so common in our culture—or the social activism that is often viewed as its alternative. It involves both spiritual formation and action for the sake of a world where everyone has enough and no one needs to be afraid. It invites us to set aside our self-interest and instead cultivate active concern for the interests of others. Faithfulness to the way of Jesus means emulating his humility through the pursuit of a cruciform life lived for the sake of others, including our enemies, as an expression of discipleship to the way of Jesus and a witness to the love of God for the healing of the world.[17]

This suggests that we will not find ultimate truth in abstract notions or theories but rather in the person of Jesus Christ and the way of life he invites us to follow. From this perspective, knowing truth and participating in truth are all-encompassing enterprises that call for an alternative lifestyle. The affirmation that Jesus is the truth is a stark challenge to the abstract ideas of truth we commonly hold. In Jesus we discover that truth is not merely intellectual but personal and relational—truth that is woven into the

17. For a development of this theme in Paul, see Michael J. Gorman, *Inhabiting the Cruciform God: Kenosis, Justification, and Theosis* (Grand Rapids: Eerdmans, 2009).

theme of love. This means that missional theology is not simply an intellectual pursuit but a holistic approach that is concerned with personal, relational, intellectual, and spiritual formation. The work of following Jesus by living God's love in the world provides solidarity for the church.

In interpreting Scripture, it is important to remember our cultural location as readers and the significance of this for the development of Christologies. They are shaped not simply by the words of the biblical texts but also by situations and challenges we perceive with respect to our social situation. This helps us to make sense of the diversity of approaches to Christology in history. Of course, the pluriform character of Christology is the result not simply of the diversity of social settings in which the gospel has been lived out and proclaimed but also of the diversity of Scripture itself.

This diversity of christological forms raises again the question of the unity of the church in the face of its differing conceptions of Jesus. If Jesus is at the center of the church, if Jesus is of ultimate significance, how are we to understand the unity of the Christian community in the midst of such diverse perspectives on Jesus? Think of the numerous and sometimes competing theories of atonement that have been part of Christian intellectual history. Put another way, how do the numerous confessions concerning Christology relate to the common confession that Jesus Christ is the one Lord of the church and the world? Does the solidarity of the church depend on arriving at a common formulation or at least an agreed-upon compromise among the many models?

From the perspective of missional theology developed here, the answer is no. Shared christological formulations may be worthwhile and significant, but they are not the basis for solidarity in the Christian community. Rather, the unity of the church is found in the living presence of Jesus promised to the Christian community and celebrated in the Eucharist, which is a symbol of the unity of the church in spite of the different ways it has been understood and practiced. It is found through participation in the mission of Jesus to forgive sins and redeem the world from sin and death.

Missional Christology does not seek a single, normative theological conception of the person and work of Christ. It acknowledges the importance of plurality in christological and theological construction while also affirming the centrality of the person of Jesus for all of life. It resists an "anything goes" approach that is characteristic of radical cultural relativism; instead, it affirms what might be called a "thick" or "convictional" plurality rooted in the Christian tradition. This thick plurality arises from the nature and character of God as a missionary, the unique role of Jesus in the mission of God, the witness of the Spirit to Jesus and the mission of God, the belief that God speaks in revelation, and the trustworthiness of Scripture as a faithful witness to that revelation.

Missional Christology is always shaped by close engagement with Scripture; but because it also is rooted in the life of local communities and particular social and cultural settings, it always will be characterized by a thick plurality arising from missional Christian convictions. This christological plurality grows out of common Christian commitments and a deep engagement with the diverse particularity and missional unity of the biblical texts. As normative witness to the person and work of Jesus Christ, these texts display christological, theological, and missional plurality. As paradigmatic witness to the person and work of Jesus Christ and to the nature and task of the church sent into mission, they invite even greater plurality in order that the fullness of the person and work of Christ may be made increasingly manifest in the witness of the church and the life of the world. In this way the church is invited into creative communal participation in the mission of God so that the good news of God's love, made known in Jesus Christ, can be extended to every tribe and nation and lived out in culturally appropriate idioms. But ultimately, the solidarity of the church is found not in these Christologies but in the living presence of Christ.

The Presence of Christ, the Work of the Spirit, and the Way of Love

While elements of commonality in theological and practical concerns, or in essential continuity, or in constants in context, or in ecumenical forms of Christology are important and instructive, they are not what draws the church together. The most significant basis for solidarity in the church is the ongoing presence of Christ and the Holy Spirit in the Christian community. We celebrate this presence in baptism and the Eucharist, which, in spite of the different ways in which these rituals have been understood and practiced, serve as symbols of the ongoing presence of Jesus with us and our solidarity with him in his mission.

As we participate in Christ's mission to redeem the world through the making of disciples, we experience the promise of his presence with us: "And remember, I am with you always, to the end of the age" (Matt. 28:19–20). The unity of the church is not to be sought by pursuing full agreement among its diverse communities on matters related to Christian teaching and practices. It is not to be found in common doctrinal statements and confessions, which—though they will remain important in the life and witness of the church—will always reflect the particular social, cultural, and historical situation of various communities throughout history, Christian or otherwise. The unity of the church, in the midst of its commitments to mission, Scripture, and particular practices, is found ultimately in the living presence of Christ promised to his followers. By the gift and witness of the Spirit, Jesus Christ is not only the example of Christian life and service but also a living presence in the midst of the Christian community. But this very presence that provides solidarity in the Christian community is experienced in diverse ways, in keeping with the missional multiplicity of the church. Theologian Thomas Oden observes:

> The circle of the Christian tradition has an unusually wide circumference without ceasing to have a single, unifying center. It

is Christ's living presence that unites a diverse tradition, yet that single presence is experienced in richly different ways. Christ's presence is experienced sacramentally by the liturgical traditions, spiritually by the charismatic traditions, as morally inspiring by the liberal traditions, as ground of social experiment by the pietistic traditions, as doctrinal teacher by the scholastic traditions, as sanctifying power of persons and society by the Greek Orthodox tradition, as grace perfecting nature by the Roman Catholic tradition, and as word of Scripture by the evangelical tradition. All of these traditions and the periods of their hegemony have experienced the living and risen Christ in spectacularly varied ways. But nothing else than the living Christ forms the center of this wide circumference.[18]

The metaphor of the church as a body helps us grasp how the many diverse experiences of the living Christ, and the historic communities of the Christian tradition that have formed around them, relate to the one, holy, catholic, and apostolic body of Christ in the world. We read that the Spirit is at work forming one body, one church, out of many parts in which a diversity of gifts are given for the edification of the whole church: "Now there are varieties of gifts, but the same Spirit; and there are varieties of services, but the same Lord; and there are varieties of activities, but it is the same God who activates all of them in everyone. To each is given the manifestation of the Spirit for the common good" (1 Cor. 12:4–7). The diversity of the church is the work of the Spirit in enabling the church to bear witness to the plurality of truth. Each part has particular gifts and contributes particular understandings of the event of truth revealed in Jesus Christ, for the edification of the whole body in service to one common Lord: "For just as the body is one and has many members, and all the members of the body, though many, are one body, so it is

18. Thomas C. Oden, *After Modernity . . . What? Agenda for Theology* (Grand Rapids: Zondervan, 1990), 176–77.

with Christ. For in the one Spirit we were all baptized into one body—Jews or Greeks, slaves or free—and we were all made to drink of one Spirit. Indeed, the body does not consist of one member but of many" (12:12–14).

In addition, the various parts of the church are interdependent. They need each other. They cannot fulfill the mission to which they are called apart from their relation to the whole body, for no single part can do all that needs to be done or comprehend all that needs to be said: "If the whole body were an eye, where would the hearing be? If the whole body were hearing, where would the sense of smell be? But as it is, God arranged the members in the body, each one of them, as he chose. If all were a single member, where would the body be? As it is, there are many members, yet one body" (12:17–20). Hence, no part of the church is independent of the rest: "If one member suffers, all suffer together with it; if one member is honored, all rejoice together with it. Now you are the body of Christ and individually members of it" (12:26–27).

This should be understood with respect to both the local church and the church universal. In the same way that various members of the local church contribute to the edification of the particular community of which they are a part, so all Christian communities should see themselves as but a part of the larger body of Christ in which each has particular gifts to bear but none is able to fulfill the missional calling and bear fully adequate witness to the plurality of truth on its own. As the metaphor of the body suggests, each of the members is dependent on the others for their overall health. The gifts, theological insights, and particular ecclesial practices provided by the Spirit to one segment of the body of Christ are intended for the benefit and edification of the whole church, but none of these are adequate for all times and places.

This serves as another caution against the temptation of a universal theology. In seeking to learn from the insights of other theological traditions and perspectives and acknowledging the significant contributions of each as they are brought to the roundtable of varying perspectives, we should expect that all theologies and traditions of reflection will be enriched. However, as Justo González reminds us, this does not mean that "what we must now do is simply bring together all the contributions of these various perspectives, in order to forge a truly 'universal' theology. Such a 'universal' theology, were it achievable, would lack true catholicity, for the same reason that a 'harmony' of the gospels, one in which all differences are resolved, must never be substituted for the fourfold witness to the gospel. When used in this manner, 'universal,' rather than a synonym for 'catholic,' is its antonym."[19] When this does occur, given how the perspective of any particular group necessarily influences its theology, claims of universality are no more than theology produced from the perspective of those who have cultural privilege.

Instead, the many parts of the church are called to participate together in a unity and a solidarity characterized by *interdependent particularity*. Each is a part, and only a part, of the embodied witness to the truth of the gospel made known in Jesus Christ. All are called to do their part in the mission of God in accordance with the particular social and historical circumstances in which they are situated and the gifting of the Spirit. All have gifts to give and to receive in the edification and building up of the one church. All are in need of the witness of the other and the discipline of critical reflection on the life and practices of the church. Plurality in the Christian community is not a problem to be overcome but is instead the very intention and blessing of God, who invites all people to participate in the liberating and reconciling ministry of the gospel of Jesus Christ. The means by which this will be accomplished follows at the conclusion of Paul's metaphor on the body, the way of love (1 Cor. 13:1–13). The end of missional theology is a community in solidarity with

19. Justo L. González, *Out of Every Tribe and Nation: Christian Theology at the Ethnic Roundtable* (Nashville: Abingdon, 1992), 26.

Jesus Christ and each other that participates in the mission of God by living God's love in and for the world. This shared participation in the mission of God, coupled with the living presence of Jesus Christ, unites diverse Christian communities throughout history and across cultures in solidarity with God, Jesus, each other, and all of creation.

Epilogue

"A world where everyone has enough and no one needs to be afraid." This phrase, repeated several times throughout this volume, is a brief summary statement for the kingdom of God intended from the beginning, initiated in the covenant with Abraham, and inaugurated in Jesus Christ. The end of missional theology is participation in turning this divine intention into a lived reality for the people of the world, a reality in which the will of God is done on earth as it is in heaven.

While missional theology can be rendered in academic or theoretical forms, which are not unimportant, such rendering can never be the end of the matter. Missional theology must be lived in the life of a community for the sake of the world. It concerns itself with formation and engagement, with the practices of hospitality, care, forgiveness, advocacy, justice, and worship. In this way, missional theology is always both practical and public: practical because it must be acted upon and lived; public because it is for the common good of all and not simply a matter of private concern among those who share its convictions.

Though missional theology is practiced and embodied in the life of the church, its intent is always beyond the horizons of the Christian community. It calls the church to look beyond itself to the common good of the larger society in which it is situated. In our pluralist and interconnected world that we share with others, the only way to ultimately establish the peace and tranquility envisioned by God in creation is to enable the flourishing of all people. Working toward the fullness of that vision is the heartbeat of missional theology. It simply points to theology done in keeping with the mission of God and the good news proclaimed by Jesus about the coming kingdom of God.

With that end in view, this volume outlines five elements of particular significance in the work of establishing this missional approach to theology. Let me briefly rehearse the contours of each as a sort of executive summary of the book.

First, it is important to offer an account of the mission and purpose of God. If—as the ecumenical, missiological consensus maintains—God is a missionary God by God's very nature, then mission no longer finds its basis in the church but in the eternal nature of God. Mission is therefore understood as a movement from God to the world, with the church functioning as a participant and witness to the mission of God. Hence, providing some account of the purposes of God stands as a necessary theological task.

The mission of God also requires articulation of the far-reaching claims that it is central for our understanding of the nature and fullness of God's purposes in the world. The divine mission is (1) at the heart of God's covenant with Israel; (2) the underlying basis for the development of Scripture as it is continuously unfolded over the centuries in the life of Israel and the early Christian community; (3) the ultimate end of the revelation of God in Jesus Christ as well as the context for his life, ministry, death, and resurrection; and (4) the basis for the continuing ministry of the Spirit, who is sent to call, guide, and empower the community of Christ's followers, the church, to be the embodied witness to the gospel of Jesus Christ and the tangible expression of the mission of God. In other words, our understanding of the mission of God shapes every aspect of Christian faith, life, thought, and witness.

Hence, this is a matter of no small consequence. Much is at stake, and different accounts of the divine mission will lead to differing conclusions about all the matters mentioned above and the approaches to theology that follow. Further, it is sometimes the case that particular notions of the divine mission function implicitly rather than explicitly. In such cases, these implicit and unspoken assumptions have a significant effect on theological assumptions but are not subjected to critical scrutiny. What I've tried to do is provide a basic sketch of the mission of God in accordance with the major themes of Scripture.

Part of the challenge here is not simply that there are a myriad of views regarding the doctrine of God but also that the Bible can be read in different and sometimes competing ways. In spite of the challenges, holding tightly to the mission of God in the world is a crucial first step in missional theology. The mission of God is rooted in the Trinity, characterized by love in the eternal life of God and salvation as that love is expressed in a created order that has rebelled against the love of God.

This salvation must not be understood from the individualistic perspective of modern Western culture, which often reduces it to the redemption of particular individuals for a heavenly future. Without denying that salvation is concerned with the redemption of individuals, such an individualistic approach fails to perceive the full scope and grandeur of the divine mission in which God acts on behalf of the whole created order to set it free from its bondage to decay. This approach also fails to perceive that the salvation God enacts is not merely a heavenly rest after death but rather a present reality for this life.

The salvation intended by God is the liberation of the whole created order, including humanity and the entire cosmos, from the powers of sin and death. Its focal point is the establishment of peace on earth. This comprehensive vision of God's salvation is captured in the language and themes of Scripture, such as liberation, transformation, new creation, peace, reconciliation, and justification. All are connected to the salvific expression of love that is at the center of the divine mission.

The second element in the development of a missional approach to theology consists of connecting the mission of God to the mission of the church. The ecumenical consensus has affirmed the inseparable link between the two, with the church participating in the broader mission of God, but it does not specify the precise nature of the church's participation. As with the articulation of the mission of God, attempts at establishing the nature of the relationship between the mission of God and the mission of the church, as well as their entailments, have also been contested and controversial. But the shared notion is that the church of the missional God revealed in Jesus Christ must itself be missional. The church must participate in the mission of God. Such participation invests the church in the movement of God's love for the world and calls forth a response of witness consistent with that movement. Missional theology asserts that God's engagement with the world arises from God's eternal character, and consequently the church of this God must relate to the world in ways consistent with the divine character and intention.

This connection between the mission of God and the mission of the church is made pointedly in John 20:21–23: "Jesus said to them again, 'Peace be with you. As the Father has sent me, so I send you.' When he had said this, he breathed on them and said to them, 'Receive the Holy Spirit. If you forgive the sins of any, they are forgiven them; if you retain the sins of any, they are retained.'" The disciples and the church are sent into the world by Jesus in the pattern by which the Father sent the Son. The followers of Jesus are called to nothing less than the communal continuation of the divine mission.

I have outlined the mission of the church using the nomenclature suggested by Lesslie Newbigin: the Christian community is a sign, an instrument, and a foretaste of the kingdom of God. And I have added a trinitarian twist: the church is called to bear the image of God as a sign of the kingdom; to be the body of Christ as an instrument of the kingdom; and to be the dwelling place of the Spirit as a foretaste of the kingdom. I have sought to connect each of these with core practices of Christian faith and mission: discipleship, evangelism, and worship.

The church is sent into the world to bear the image of God as a sign of the divine kingdom through discipleship in the way of Jesus; to be the body of Christ as an instrument of the kingdom of God by proclaiming and establishing that kingdom through holistic evangelism; and to be the dwelling place of the Spirit and a foretaste of the kingdom by living together in community and worshiping God. However, this activity is always incarnational and contextual, embodied in ways that reflect the particular times and places in which it is enacted. In its responsiveness to place and particularity, it becomes pluriform rather than uniform. Missional theology invites the church to break from the patterns of colonization that have all too often characterized its approach to mission throughout history with tragic consequences that are inimical to the mission of God.

The third element in the development of a missional approach to theology involves recasting our understanding of theology so that it serves the mission of God and the participation of the church in that mission while resisting patterns of cultural imperialism and colonization. The assumptions and intuitions that continue to shape the work of theology still tend to be those of Christendom rather than of the mission of God. Further, even when mission plays a more substantial role in a particular theology, it generally functions as a discrete component in a larger picture rather than an integrative motif for the whole. The challenge is to move from theology with a mission component to a truly missional conception of theology, in which mission is at the center of theological discourse. Such an approach will take seriously the implications

of place and context and be oriented toward the life and witness
of the church, particularly with respect to its practical and public
manifestations.

To help facilitate this recasting I have defined missional theology
as an ongoing, second-order, contextual discipline that engages in
the task of critical and constructive reflection on the beliefs and
practices of the Christian church for the purpose of assisting the
community of Christ's followers in their missional vocation to live
as the people of God in their particular social-historical context.

The process of doing missional theology starts in the life and
witness of a community that believes in the gospel and is prepared
to live by it. As the community bears witness to the gospel in its
particular setting, it has encounters and experiences that continually shape and challenge its conception of the gospel. These lived
encounters and experiences provide the starting point for cultural
and theological reflection, which in turn leads to missional action
as the community and the individuals within it determine how
they will respond to those particular situations and challenges.
This approach strongly emphasizes the significance of place and
particularity in the work of theology.

In this local and radically contextual model of theology, the
Christian tradition is best understood as a series of local translations of the gospel that lead to particular iterations of Christian
communal life and witness based on the texts of Scripture in relationship to particular social, historical, and cultural conditions.
This pluriform tradition is visible in the history of biblical interpretation, preaching, theology, worship, and mission; past theological formulations such as confessions and creeds, and the faith
expressions of individuals; and the expansion and development
of Christianity as a world movement. All of these bear witness
to the infinite translatability of the gospel and its relevance for all
situations and circumstances.

The fourth element is that of providing a theological account
of the missional multiplicity that follows from the theological

procedures described in chapter 3. For some, this may be the most challenging part of this proposal. I would suggest that if this is true, it is indicative of how the intuitions of Christendom remain deeply imbedded in the imagination of the Christian community. This is perhaps understandable since the church has lived with those intuitions for so much of its history. On the other hand, these intuitions, having so often distorted the gospel proclaimed by Jesus into an instrument of manipulation and oppression, ought to have alerted the church to some of their fundamental difficulties. And in spite of attempts to suppress appropriate multiplicity in the life of the church, it is plurality rather than uniformity that characterizes the story of Christianity.

To develop this notion of plurality I have provided a brief description of a threefold understanding of the Word of God. It is always an *act* God performs or an *event* in which God has spoken, speaks, and will speak. As human beings, we encounter and engage this divine act or event through Scripture (Spirit-inspired) and its proclamation and practice in the life of the church (Spirit-guided). The event of the Word of God has three forms: the act of revelation itself, the Spirit-inspired attestation and witness to revelation in the words of Scripture, and the Spirit-guided proclamation of that witness in the life of the church.

As churches from every tribe and nation receive and interact with the Word of God throughout time and place, it follows that Christian faith is not culturally or theologically uniform, but rather characterized by cultural, theological, and missional dynamism and diversity in its witness to the gospel. Christian multiplicity is not primarily the result of human failure, though regrettably there have been many instances of inappropriate hostility and fragmentation. Though unfortunate, these instances do not constitute the ultimate basis for the diversity of the church. The church looks the way it does—diverse and pluriform—because this is the intention of God. This irreducible plurality reflects the missional nature of the Christian community bearing witness to the gospel among all peoples and situations. This has produced, and will continue to produce, the missional multiplicity that is the very nature and essence of the Christian faith.

This book maintains that the shape of an appropriately missional theology should be characterized by four traits: it is dialogical, open and committed to the other, beyond foundations, and against totality. Such a theology will work to preserve and promote the multiplicity of the church and its theological perspectives in accordance with the mission of God, in which pluralism is the cornerstone of the universal design.

The fifth element in establishing this missional approach to theology involves providing some account of missional solidarity amid the pluralism intended by God. If the witness of the church is, and must be, characterized by plurality and multiplicity, how are we to understand the unity of the church? How can we conceive of the unity of the Christian community in a diverse church embodied throughout history in a dazzling array of forms? Even as Scripture bears witness to the polyphonic character of the one faith, it also proclaims the unity of the church. In response to the danger of plurality and freedom turning into strife and violence, both the Hebrew Bible and the New Testament promote the goodness and importance of unity. But where is this unity and solidarity to be found?

Some have asserted that this unity may be found in the shared doctrinal and ecclesial commitments of the historic Christian faith. However, this notion seems problematic in relation to both the actual diversity of the faith throughout history as well as the means by which Christendom was able to secure the unity that it managed to forge. A unity based on pragmatism, power, and coercion is not the oneness for which Jesus prays in John 17. We do find a basis for commonality in certain respects related to the historical connection among Christian communities, an essential continuity in some matters of shared practice, and a basic commitment to the lordship of Jesus.

Though the commonality found in theological and practical concerns, essential continuity, and ecumenical teaching on Christology are instructive, I suggest that the most significant basis for solidarity in the church is to be found ultimately in the ongoing presence of Christ, the ministry of the Holy Spirit, participation in the mission of God, and the way of love. As we participate in Christ's mission to redeem the world through the individual and communal self-sacrificing love, we experience the promise of his presence with us. By the gift and witness of the Spirit, Jesus Christ is not only the example of Christian life and service but also a living presence in the Christian community. Yet this very presence, which provides solidarity in the Christian community, is also experienced in diverse ways in keeping with the missional multiplicity of the church.

The interdependent particularity that emerges from shared solidarity in Christ frees the churches of every time and place to fully participate in the mission of God and offer their distinctive witness to the gospel of Jesus Christ. No single individual, church, community, or denomination is able to say all that needs to be said or do all that needs to be done. It is only through the collective work and witness of the whole that the intentions of God are realized and made visible in the world. We cannot bear this witness alone. We were never intended to do so. We need each other. It cannot be otherwise. We are called to bear the image of the triune God in the world as a sign, instrument, and foretaste of God's kingdom.

While I believe that these five elements provided here offer a substantial introduction to missional theology, I am also aware that much more can and should be said at every point. Perhaps some of these elements need to be refuted and corrected (don't all stand up at once). Doubtless much needs to be further developed and substantiated. Much more work needs to be done if the so-called missional turn is to be established in the church and the academy. From my perspective, much of the initial enthusiasm that greeted the advent of the missional church movement has been lost due to the relative lack of theological engagement. With some exceptions, much of the conversation has become little more than another pragmatic effort at church growth. This might explain why many people believe that the missional movement has come and gone.

Of course, I don't believe that. Doing theology for the mission of God has the potential to reform the church again and again, calling it to ever-increasing faithfulness in its witness to the gospel and its participation in the mission of God. It invites all people, from every tribe and nation, into the grand conversation of theology with a deep awareness that everyone has a stake in its direction and all have contributions that the church and the world need to hear. As voices old and new share in this ongoing work, everything is refreshed and made new. This inclusive openness is central to the practice of missional theology. It is also the necessary starting point for the realization of a world where everyone has enough and no one needs to be afraid.

Index